GOD'S CALL↓NG

IT'S FOR YOU

RONNIE DAUBER

Printed in the United States of America 2016

All scriptures referenced in this book are quoted directly from the King
James Bible, unless otherwise specified.

Author Credits:
NO Compromise, Biblical Answers to Some of Today's Issues (2015)
Let Faith Arise (first edition 2012)
Let Faith Arise (second edition 2016)

Books may be ordered through booksellers or by contacting:
Create Space
http://www.createspace.com

or

Ronnie Dauber website
http://www.ronniedauber.ca

ISBN-978-0-9949370-1-8

Contents

Acknowledgements

I want to thank my husband and best friend, Eric Dauber, for his encouragement and support throughout the duration of writing this book. He understands the importance of helping others to find God and has been my greatest motivation.

I also want to thank my dear friend and professional graphic designer and illustrator, Mishel McCumber, for her time and dedication to this project. She has prayerfully designed the perfect book cover to portray the message within its pages.

And I want to give all my praise and thanks to our Lord and God for inspiring me to write this book and for giving me the heart and insight to the messages that people so desperately need to hear. Jesus is the reason that I say, "Smile, God Loves You!"

Introduction

In this ever-changing world of amazing technology, modified ethics and revised laws, we can include a platform of "Christian" doctrines that add a religious freedom to the modern-day changes. They all proclaim to be the way to find God and people are being deceived into believing that all they have to do is pick the one that suits them best and then that makes them a Christian. But this is a blatant lie! It defies scripture and is leading many to hell. God is calling all sinners to repentance, and He is calling YOU! Will you answer God's call?

False doctrines are spreading like wildfire across the globe because it's easier for people to follow a doctrine that caters to their fleshly desires than to one that requires repentance and change. People want God's blessings now and they want a home in Heaven later on, but they don't want to change or give up their comfortable lifestyle—and they don't want to hear about repentance. They want their god to be one who loves and accepts them just as they are.

False doctrines are subtle and deceiving. They remove the emphasis of Christianity, which is repentance, forgiveness and submission to the holiness of God, and place it onto the people for their own reward. They teach that God is changing to accommodate today's world, that scriptures are up to personal interpretation and that it's perfectly legal for the religious leaders to change the scriptures to meet modern-day standards. It encourages people to listen to the voice inside their heart so they can hear new revelations instead of reading the Bible. Deception is calling people onto the path of destruction.

This book is filled with inspirational messages that deal with the many ways people are missing the truth about God, ways that are subtle and deceiving. Many people believe that they're on the right path, and that's what deception does; it misleads. It came to Eve in the Garden of Eden and deceived her into thinking that eating the fruit would make her as smart as God. She was wrong and because she convinced Adam to eat the fruit as well, his actions brought sin upon all of mankind. But Jesus has paid the price for those sins with His life, and only those who accept it and follow Him will be redeemed back to God.

People need to close their eyes to the deception of false, enticing doctrines that cater to the flesh, and they need to stop looking at themselves in the mirror and priding themselves of their faith. It's time for people to become humble and realize that if Jesus isn't in the centre of their being, then they need to repent! It's time to get wise to the sins of heretic doctrines.

And ye shall know the truth, and the truth shall make you free.—John 8:32

The Bible is our only source of truth because it is the inspired word of God—2 Timothy 3:16. We need to read it prayerfully and allow God's Spirit to reveal its powerful message to us. We can't cherry pick what scriptures suit us because God is the same yesterday, today and forever— Hebrews 13:8. We either accept all of the truth and live it now or deny it and get judged by Him later.

For it is written, 'As I live', saith the Lord, 'every knee shall bow to me, and every tongue shall confess to God'.—Romans 14:11

We need to be wise and search for the truth in the scriptures! The Bible is the only source of truth. It is not conflicting or confusing. It is written in perfect harmony and reveals to us God's full plan.

There is only one way to Heaven and that is through Jesus! There are no alternative paths and no one can do it for you! Every person ever born needs to come to Yeshua and repent of their sins, accept Him as the Lamb of God who shed His blood for their sins and then get filled with His Holy Spirit. Only then can we say that we are His redeemed. Old Testament believers were saved by their faith and obedience to God (Yeshua); New Testament believers are saved by their faith and obedience through the grace of God (Yeshua).

> Neither is there salvation in any other: for there is none other name under heaven given among men, whereby we must be saved.— Acts 4:12

Time is running out and Jesus (Yeshua) our King will soon come! He is calling sinners to repentance. Now is the time to find Him and accept His forgiveness for sin.

It's the hope and prayers of this author that you will read this book and be encouraged to study the Bible yourself so you can hear His voice and know the truth.

God is calling and He wants YOU to follow Him!

The Broad Way to Destruction Widens

There are modern-day "Christian" doctrines that teach God is a god of "love and grace", and that repentance and commitment are no longer prerequisites to get into Heaven because we were all saved at the cross when Jesus said, "It is finished"—(John 19:30). However, this deception is leading millions down the wrong path...and so the broad path to destruction widens!

When Jesus said "It is finished", He was referring to the plan of salvation that God had promised Adam and Eve; the one that would crush the head of the serpent, the devil. The Old Testament is a book of law, prophesy and history, and the New Testament is the fulfillment of those prophesies about the coming Messiah, Jesus our Savior. God's plan was finished! The provision for salvation was completed and was now available to all of mankind.

> For God so loved the world that He gave His only begotten Son, that whosoever believeth in Him should not perish, but have everlasting life.—John 3:16

He didn't say that everyone is automatically saved; He said that He loved all of mankind and that He wanted them all to be saved. He has called every person to come to the cross and receive His salvation, yet only a few will accept it. Matthew 22:14 says, "For many are called, but few are chosen." The provision is for everyone, but only those who come to the cross, repent and receive Jesus as their Savior, and then turn from the world to follow Him will be saved and will go to Heaven when they leave earth.

> Not everyone that saith unto me, 'Lord, Lord', shall enter into the kingdom of heaven;

Ronnie Dauber

but he that doeth the will of My Father which
is in Heaven.—Matthew 7:21

Today's lifestyle is all about "me"! It's about
convenience, pleasure, riches and self accomplishment. It's
about living in sin while at the same time conceding to that
tiny voice of guilt that says, "I need some kind of religion to
ensure I get into Heaven when I die." And so many
ignorantly go along with whatever is being taught, just as
long as they think that they'll get into Heaven—and without
having to read the Bible to get there.

> This know also, that in the last days perilous
> times shall come. 2 For men shall be lovers of
> their own selves, covetous, boasters, proud,
> blasphemers, disobedient to parents,
> unthankful, unholy, 3 Without natural
> affection, trucebreakers, false accusers,
> incontinent, fierce, despisers of those that are
> good, 4 Traitors, heady, high-minded, lovers
> of pleasures more than lovers of God;
> 5 Having a form of godliness, but denying the
> power thereof: from such turn away.—2
> Timothy 3:1-5

The new age message says that we are all God's
children. But we are NOT all God's children! Only those
who have come to the cross and accepted Jesus as their Lord,
Savior and King, and who have repented of their sins are part
of the Kingdom of God. Those who don't come to the cross
and repent still belong to this sinful world. They don't have
the Spirit of God in them because they are not born again—
John 3:3.

This modern-day "love" doctrine doesn't preach the
gospel of Christ, but rather, that we need to love all people
and that we should not judge or criticize anyone regardless of

2

their actions or lifestyles. It has taken the scripture from Mark 12:31 that says we need to love our neighbor as our self, and it has turned these words into a false doctrine that promotes the love of people above the love of God. It says that we need to see everyone as saved and that we should not even be concerned over any sin that anyone promotes because all sin is under the blood and forgiven.

God says clearly that we need to be born again and that we are to love the brethren—but all of humanity is not "the brethren". Only those who are born again are brethren. Jesus says that His beloved are those who love Him.

> While He yet talked to the people, behold, His mother and His brethren stood without, desiring to speak with Him. 47 Then one said unto Him, 'Behold, thy mother and thy brethren stand without, desiring to speak with thee.' 48 But He answered and said unto him that told Him, 'Who is my mother? And who are my brethren?' 49 And He stretched forth His hand toward His disciples, and said, 'Behold, my mother and my brethren! 50 For whosoever shall do the will of My Father which is in Heaven, the same is My brother, and sister, and mother.'—Matthew 12:47-50

God hates sin and has condemned all sin to hell— Romans 6:23, and as Christians we have compassion for the sinful people of the world, but it's not the same as the love we feel for our brothers and sisters in Christ. In the same light, we may have compassion for our acquaintances and our neighbors, but it's not the same as the love and devotion we have for our own family. We want those who are lost to be saved, but their sin separates us because we can't have fellowship with anyone who willfully engages in sin. God hates sin, and we who are filled with His spirit will also hate

3

sin. We won't accept it or condone it, but rather, we won't want to be around it.

> Be ye not unequally yoked together with unbelievers: for what fellowship hath righteousness with unrighteousness? And what communion hath light with darkness?— 2 Corinthians 6:14

> And have no fellowship with the unfruitful works of darkness, but rather reprove them.— Ephesians 5:11

> If we say that we have fellowship with Him, and walk in darkness, we lie, and do not the truth: 7 But if we walk in the light, as He is in the light, we have fellowship one with another, and the blood of Jesus Christ, His Son, cleanseth us from all sin.—1 John 1:6-7

Sadly, many are deceived by this false teaching and believe that God doesn't want or expect them to change. He just wants them to love each other and enjoy their life on earth just as they are because He loves them just as they are. They believe that repentance is not necessary and that salvation is automatically for everyone, and so it's not to be made into a personal thing. They take the words of John 3:16 that say, "For God so loved the world that He gave His only begotten Son" to mean that Jesus died for everyone and there is nothing that anyone has to do to receive salvation. And so, the broad way to destruction widens because deception is keeping people from the narrow path that leads to truth.

> Enter ye in at the strait gate: for wide is the gate, and broad is the way that leadeth to destruction, and many there be which go in thereat: 14Because strait is the gate, and

narrow is the way, which leadeth unto life and
few there be that find it.—Matthew 7:13-14

The way that leads to God is narrow and has only one
doorway that takes us to God, and that door is Christ Jesus.
And all those who enter will be saved and will have
everlasting life with God. But the key is that you have to
enter through Christ to get there, not through a doctrine that
deceives.

I am the door: by me if any man enter in, he
shall be saved, and shall go in and out, and
find pasture.—John 10:9

He's a God of Love AND Hate

The New Age religion wants us to believe that God is all about love and that He doesn't hate anything or anyone. It wants us to accept that He forgave the sins of every person ever born when He died on the cross, and that repentance is a religious works and not a submission of the heart. It wants us to think that God loves everyone for who they are and that they don't have to change a thing to get into Heaven. What a lie! Yes, God loves us, but the Bible says clearly that there are seven things God hates!

Proverbs 6:16-19 NKJV says:

These six things the Lord hates, Yes, seven are an abomination to Him:

A proud look, A lying tongue, Hands that shed innocent blood, A heart that devises wicked plans, Feet that are swift in running o evil, A false witness who speaks lies, And one who sows discord among brethren.

We were all guilty of these sins before we knew the Lord, but once we are saved we are forgiven for them and we are not to continue in them. God tells us clearly in 2 Corinthians 6:17 that we are to "come out from among them and be separate." Yet, there are so-called Christians among us who still engage in them and believe that it's okay. But it's foolish to assume that it's okay instead of studying the Bible and knowing what God has done for us and what He expects of us. We can know what things God hates and what He doesn't want us to do.

A proud look: The opposite of pride is humility, and God tells us to humble ourselves before Him and to treat our brethren with love so we can have peace among us in spite of our differences.—Ephesians 4:1-3. Pride is the evidence of

6

what is most dear to the heart and it's reflected in our appearance and in our attitude. It promotes a self-appointed god, and Exodus 20:3 says that we should have no other gods before the God of Heaven.

> Humble yourselves in the sight of the Lord,
> and He will lift you up.—James 4:10

A lying tongue: God hates lies and He hates liars. We are not only told in the Ten Commandments that lying is a sin, but Jesus clearly tells us in the New Testament that people who lie are still under the influence of this world's god, the devil. We cannot belong to God and to the devil. If we belong to God then we cannot lie because His Holy Spirit in us will convict us before we get the lie out. And for new or weak Christians, the second they do lie they will be convicted and will immediately repent.

> You are of your father the devil, and the desires of your father you want to do.....When he speaks a lie, he speaks from his own resources, for he is a liar and the father of it.—John 8:44 NKJV

Hands that shed innocent blood: God told us that we are not to kill—Exodus 20:13. Every life to Him is precious and no one has the right to take a life except Him. And yet, thousands of innocent lives are being taken every day—legal murders called "abortions". It's become a normal "procedure" and to avoid the issue or conviction of it being murder, the babies are referred to as "fetus" instead of an innocent child. But the world's acceptance of this hideous crime does not change the fact that it's murder! The cries of these children rise up to Heaven every day, and although the world has made it legal, God has not changed. He has always hated murder beginning with the very first one committed by Cain, and this sin will not go without His judgment upon every single person who engages in this unspeakable sin.

> You are of your father the devil, and the desires of your father you want to do. He was a murderer from the beginning, and does not stand in the truth, because there is no truth in him.—John 8:44 NKJV

A heart that devices wicked plans: We see wicked plans in the acts of terrorism around us and we're appalled, but that same attitude is also there in the business world, in government offices and in personal lives. When we become a Christian, our old self dies with all of its wickedness and we become born again with God's Spirit. There is no sin or desire to fulfill sin in our heart and therefore, we yearn only to do the things of God and to please Him. Our heart wants to love and serve God, to love our brethren, and to show Jesus to the world. The only plans we have are ones that bring glory to God, and if not then we need to get into the Bible and find out what our motive is and who we are trying to please; the God of Heaven or the god of this world.

> The steps of a good man are ordered by the Lord, And He delights in his way.—Psalm 37:23 NKJV

Feet that are swift in running to evil: When we become a Christian our thoughts and values change and we lose the desire to hang out with our old friends who are still part of the sinful world. We won't want to go to the places or do the things that we once craved, and that separates us from our old friends and from worldly activities. We now find them very wrong and that's because Christ has put new desires in our heart. We only want to go to places that please the Lord. Now our feet are blessed and they go where Christ leads us and where He will be glorified.

Stand therefore, having your loins girt about
with truth, and having on the breastplate of
righteousness; 15 And your feet shod with the
preparation of the gospel of peace.—
Ephesians 6:14-15

A false witness who speaks lies: God says in Exodus
20:16 that we are not to bear false witness against our
neighbor, and in Exodus 23:1 He says that we are not to raise
a false report against anyone. In Deuteronomy 19 God says
that anyone who gives a false witness is to be put out from
among the people. And yet, many people feel justified to give
false witness in the courtroom and in the work place, and it's
even done by children in the classroom. A modern-day word
for this is "gossip" and this is very common in today's world
for friends and groups of friends to gossip and tear down
each other. It may be done in ignorance as a child, but how
devastating it becomes as adults when gossip turns into
destruction. God tells us to speak only on things that uplift
and bring glory to Him—Philippians 4:8.

A false witness shall not be unpunished, and
he that speaketh lies shall not escape.—
Proverbs 19:5

And one who sows discord among the brethren: Just
as Jesus said would happen, the leaders of many of our
churches are calling themselves Christians, but are serving
people instead of following Him. Some support the
perversion of homosexuality—1 Corinthians 6:9, and others
employ female pastors contrary to what God said in 1
Timothy 2:11-14. And still others are false preachers
who blatantly promote false doctrines rather than the gospel
of Jesus. These acts of disobedience are causing discord and
division in the church body because some members want to
hold fast to the real gospel and others want a new and more
permissible gospel. And so the true believers become less

9

and less and the false ones grow in number because the world has such a strong affect on lifestyle, that many so-called Christians want to join in with the new version of Christianity—and it's being done in the name of Jesus.

> But there were also false prophets among the people, even as there will be false teachers among you, who will secretly bring in destructive heresies, even denying the Lord who bought them, and bring on themselves swift destruction.—2 Peter 2:1 NKJV

God is the epitome of love as He showed us so clearly on the cross, but He also hates sin. And one day He will cast sin into the Lake of Fire to burn forever. We need to study the scriptures so we can know how to please God and how, as disciples of Christ, we can live and represent the truth in everything we do!

> Let the words of my mouth, and the meditation of my heart, be acceptable in thy sight, O Lord, my strength, and my redeemer.—Psalm 19:14

A Dark Hour is Coming

It seems that life now-a-days has more ups and downs and constant challenges than ever before. The law has changed dramatically and now it allow things that years ago would have been forbidden such as the legalization of abortion and the acceptance of a homosexual lifestyle. Crime and pointless killings have become a normal part of life, sickness and incurable diseases are on the rise, and God has been eliminated from public sectors such as schools, work places – and even churches! The security of every person on earth is being contested, and we'll see that not too far in the future those who don't know Christ will face a very dark hour.

We have watched the chaos unravel around us for years and now we see the dangers they all present and the future that we face. Many of us are scared. What is our hope for the future?

While it is true that the world is becoming overrun by sin, it is also true that as Christians we belong to Christ and this world is not our home. So this world with its sin does not control us. When we were born again, Jesus became the Lord over our life and we did that when we walked away from darkness into His light, from this world into His kingdom. And so we have to realize that HE is in control of everything that happens in our life, and we can know His leadership when we study our Bible and follow Him and trust Him. The world will continue down its path of destruction, but we will keep our eyes on Jesus and follow Him on the narrow path.

Enter ye in at the strait gate: for wide is the gate, and broad is the way that leadeth to destruction, and many there be which go in there at: 14 Because strait is the gate, and narrow is the way, which leadeth unto life,

11

and few there be that find it.—Matthew 7:13-14

In Matthew 24:3, the disciples came to Jesus and asked Him, "Tell us, when shall these things be and what shall be the sign of thy coming, and of the end of the world?" Jesus answered them in verses 4-14 and explained what signs to look for, and then in verses 15-51 He went into more detail about what things would happen in the last days before He would return. These scriptures no longer refer to the "future" of mankind because we now live in the time when we can see evidence of many of these occurrences.

And we are not far from the time that is spoken of in Luke 21:26 when we're told about the fear that would come to mankind because of these events. "Men's hearts failing them for fear, and for looking after those things which are coming on the earth: for the powers of heaven shall be shaken."

The world is literally falling apart, yet many will argue and say that Christianity is spreading across the globe more now than ever before in history and that we're entering a time of revival. However, while it's true that Christianity is being preached all around the world by many born-again believers who have devoted their lives to spreading the gospel of Christ, there are even more who are spreading a false doctrine of Christ. Not everyone who says they are a Christians is, in fact, a Christian.

Much of the so-called Christian world, as we know it in general today, is not led by Jesus or founded on the real gospel of Jesus according to the scriptures. It's a false gospel that caters to the desires of people—aka lusts of the flesh—and does not teach the true gospel of Christ. There are many false preachers and religions that make people feel good and that seem to hit right on with what they want to believe. And since the churches they join are called "churches"—be it physical congregations or television evangelical organizations—they feel secure in their ignorance. They think they're safe, but don't realize that they are being deceived and are on the road to hell.

These false preachers, teachers and prophets will all face the judgment of God one day and be cast into hell because they deceived the people into straying from the Bible, and in the name of Christ they taught a false gospel. And each person who follows them and agrees with them will also stand before God and face punishment because they chose to cater to their flesh rather than search the scriptures and know the truth.

> But there were false prophets also among the people, even as there shall be false teachers among you, who privily shall bring in damnable heresies, even denying the Lord that bought them, and bring upon themselves swift destruction.—2 Peter 2:1

As we read in Matthew 7, there are many false preachers and doctrines that the devil has cleverly planted here just to deceive people and keep them from knowing God. The less of God there is in this world, the more the devil can rule in lawlessness and the more damage he can do. When people carelessly assume that they will go to Heaven and that God will protect them and give them everything they want and feel that they deserve here on earth, they are fools. Satan has used the false leaders to deceive them, and when they leave this earth and face God, they will receive their judgment right along with the deceivers who they followed.

> Many will say to me in that day, 'Lord, Lord, have we not prophesied in thy name? And in thy name have cast out devils? And in thy

name done many wonderful works?' 23 And
then will I profess unto them, 'I never knew
you: depart from me, ye that work
iniquity'.—Matthew 7:22-23

A very dark hour is coming upon this earth, just as
Jesus said, and the only way we will get through it is with
Him. Though many Christians hope to be "raptured" and
escape the Great Tribulation, we see in the Bible that we will
likely go through it because everything in the New Testament
about the end of days and the tribulation is parallel with the
exodus of the children of Israel from their enslavement in
Egypt. This is where blood from chosen lambs was placed on
the doorposts as atonement for their sins to protect them from
the plague of death was to come upon that nation. And it will
be the same during the tribulation; we have the blood of
Jesus over us to protect us from the wrath to come. No one
knows when that day will be, but all the signs tell us that it's
coming soon.

Immediately after the tribulation of those days shall
the sun be darkened, and the moon shall not give her light,
and the stars shall fall from heaven, and the powers of the
heavens shall be shaken: 30 And then shall appear the sign of
the Son of man in heaven: and then shall all the tribes of the
earth mourn, and they shall see the Son of man coming in the
clouds of heaven with power and great glory. 31 And He
shall send His angels with a great sound of a trumpet, and
they shall gather together His elect from the four winds, from
one end of heaven to the other.—Matthew 24:29-31

False Christianity and ignorance might get us riches
and fame here on earth, but it will not cause us to escape
God's wrath that is coming—and that has already begun. Life
is not about what we can get from God now so we can have it
all here; life is about being redeemed from this world of sin
and serving Christ now, and being blessed with the rewards

of our labor when we get to Heaven. And if we are not born again and filled with God's Sprit, then we are still filled with sin and we still belong to this world. And as we read in Romans 6:23, the wages of sin is death.

No one knows when they will die, and medicine and modern science can only sustain life for so long. We will all leave our bodies one day and face God. Don't be fooled into thinking that you can accept Jesus and change your lifestyle on that day when His presence convicts us of His truth because the opportunities for salvation happen on earth, not at Heaven's door. It's too late to accept Christ then.

> There shall be weeping and gnashing of teeth, when ye shall see Abraham, and Isaac, and Jacob, and all the prophets, in the kingdom of God, and you yourselves thrust out.—Luke 13:28

When we live for Jesus, He leads us and guides us and is with us through everything that comes against us. We will experience a blessed peace in our heart because of the love of God that lives in us; a love that gives us the strength to carry out the great commission of Jesus—is to preach the gospel. We won't fear because regardless of what happens here on earth we have a home in Heaven where our Heavenly Father waits for us. But those who don't know Jesus will soon know what fear is because a very dark hour is coming.

> Behold, the hour cometh, yea, is now come, that ye shall be scattered, every man to his own, and shall leave me alone: and yet I am not alone, because the Father is with me. These things I have spoken unto you, that in me ye might have peace. In the world ye shall have tribulation: but be of good cheer; I have overcome the world.—John 16:32-33

Abused for Personal Gain

Nothing excites the heart more than love. Nothing quiets anxiety more than love. And nothing gives us the confidence to endure trials and temptations more than love. Life is all about God's love for us as proven by the salvation He gave to us on the cross. Yet, many people don't know God because they only hear that God loves them and wants to bless them, and so they focus only on the blessings that He will give them here on earth. They foolishly take the intent of God's love and make it a venue for personal gain.

Much of today's church is still falling into the prosperity message rather than the gospel message. Instead of teaching repentance and salvation, it's pushing its own doctrine; a message of love and prosperity; a message that says God wants us to be wealthy here on earth because He loves us. It teaches that once we're saved God will bless us with riches, good health, constant blessings and freedom from tribulations and all we have to do is plant financial seeds to build our faith. This, however, is not Christianity; it's a false doctrine that is deceiving many by using scriptures to promote its own agenda.

It's not God's hand that we should seek after, but His face. When we come to the cross and accept His salvation, we need to understand why He did this for us. It wasn't so we could gain riches in a sinful world that waits to be judged, but so that we could escape the judgment that's coming upon it! God loves us enough to die and give us this life, and it's a life that will continue on throughout eternity and not end with destruction.

> For God so loved the world, that He gave His only begotten Son, that whosoever believeth in Him should not perish, but have everlasting life. 17 For God sent not his Son into the

world to condemn the world; but that the
world through Him might be saved.—John
3:16-17

God's love for us is more than most people can
comprehend. There's not one person on earth who could ever
have done what Jesus did for us. He left His throne in
Heaven to come to sinful earth and become a man to live a
transient life with no physical possessions, not even His own
tent to hide in from the endless persecution He endured.
Then He offered His body as a sacrifice for our sins, and was
nailed to the cross so He could take on those sins and redeem
us back to our Heavenly Father. And He did this for every
sinner, many of whom weren't even born yet. This is truly an
amazing love!

Greater love hath no man than this, that a man
lay down His life for His friends.—John
15:13

This modern-day doctrine encourages people to seed
finances in faith so they have the blessings that God's wants
them to have as their inheritance now. Yet, God clearly tells
us in 1 Peter 1:4 that Heaven is our inheritance, not anything
here on earth. And sadly, many people who follow these false
doctrines actually think they are Christians, but they aren't.
They only focus on lusts and desires and things they can get
from God, but they don't want to know Him beyond that or
change or serve Him as their Lord. They never really grasp
what the cross is all about and never seek to know Him
beyond what they can get from Him. If they did read the
Bible, they would surely know that their doctrine is a lie.

What are Christians? They are people who believe
that Jesus Christ is the Son of God who left Heaven to
become a man, died on the cross for our sins, was buried and
rose again, and now sits on the right hand of God in Heaven.

Christians are people who have repented of their sins, accepted Christ as their Messiah and come out of the world to follow Him. They are people who carry on His great commission to spread the truth about Jesus so others can get saved, and they are people whose heart is to serve Christ because they love Him, and not the desires of the flesh.

Being a Christian means that we are free of the sinful nature that we were physically born with and that we are now "saved" from the judgment that God will enforce on the people of this earth who follow after its sinful ways and who don't accept Jesus as their Lord and Savior. It means being covered by the righteous blood of Christ and that our name is written in the Book of Life so we can be with Him forever.

> And whosoever was not found written in the Book of Life was cast into the lake of fire.— Revelation 20:15

We know from Romans 6:23 that the wages of sin is death—eternal separation from God—and it was never God's intention that a single person should ever go to hell. And once sin entered man, He gave them a choice to keep the sin or repent from it. When we choose to not accept His salvation, or choose to follow a false gospel instead of the truth, it's a choice that we make and we will live to regret it throughout eternity. But it is not God's will for us.

> The Lord is not slack concerning His promise, as some men count slackness; but is longsuffering to us-ward, not willing that any should perish, but that all should come to repentance.—2 Peter 3:9

God's love saved us from the judgment to come and made us part of His family so that we can live with Him throughout eternity. We have a wonderful future with Jesus where we will live, love and laugh forever. This hope and the presence of His Spirit in us now keeps us alive and gives us the strength to endure life here on earth until we will go to be with Him.

> In my Father's house are many mansions: if it were not so, I would have told you. I go to prepare a place for you. 3 And if I go and prepare a place for you, I will come again, and receive you unto myself; that where I am, there ye may be also.—John 14:2-3

People abuse the cross—in fact, they blaspheme the cross when in His name they proclaim to be Christians, and yet all they want is to enjoy the pleasures of this world now and teach that if we had faith, we would never endure tribulations. But Jesus never said that life would be easy if we follow Him. He said that we will have tribulation, but that we would overcome them through Him.

> These things I have spoken unto you, that in me ye might have peace. In the world ye shall have tribulation: but be of good cheer; I have overcome the world.—John 16:33

We live in a corrupt world, surrounded with sin and ungodliness. We face many of the same issues that any other person living on earth faces simply because we're here. We'll get sick, have lack of finances, suffer tragedies and experience conflicts just like anyone else. But, we have Jesus to help us through them and to protect us during them, and we have the wisdom and knowledge through studying the scriptures under His Spirit to know and trust God with them.

When we're ill we can believe God for healing because He told us in Isaiah 53:5 that "with His stripes we are healed." When we have physical needs, we know from

Philippians 4:19 that God supplies all of our needs. He even enjoys giving gifts to us just as any earthly father does—but they are gifts, not a doctrine where we demand them.

> Delight thyself also in the Lord and He shall give thee the desires of thine heart.—Psalm 37:4

> And this is the confidence that we have in Him, that if we ask any thing according to His will, He heareth us:—1 John 5:14

The key is to ask according to His will and not according to what we want. When we become Christians we serve Jesus; He does not serve us. When our mentality is set to get all we can from God now that we're saved—our earthly inheritance—we are missing God totally and need to go back to the cross and start again. Our inheritance as God's children is eternity with Jesus; it's the reward that God has for us in Heaven. It has nothing to do with possessions or status in this world.

> Knowing that of the Lord ye shall receive the reward of the inheritance: for ye serve the Lord Christ.—Colossians 3:24

Any doctrine that preaches only that God loves us and wants to bless us now is a false doctrine! We need to take our eyes off of our self and put them onto the King of Kings because He is returning very soon and we need to be ready to receive Him. And we can't do that if the selfishness of our heart is abusing God's love for us.

> Looking for that blessed hope, and the glorious appearing of the great God and our Saviour Jesus Christ.—Titus 2:13

Batteries Not Included

It is truly wonderful when someone accepts the Lord as their Savior and gives up their old way of life to follow Jesus. The Bible says in Luke 15:10 that "there is joy in the presence of the angels of God over one sinner that repents!" Yet, many will come to the cross and seemingly get saved, but will quickly return to the world. Perhaps they didn't realize that with this gift, batteries were not included.

Many new believers don't understand that Christianity is a life-long commitment and not just a one-time "give your heart to the Lord and forget it" event. They come to a point in their lives when they realize God is real and that they want to go to Heaven when they die. In that moment when they face this truth, they say the sinner's prayer and believe that they are saved; that they are Christians. But that's as far as they go. They don't read the Bible or attend church or pursue God in any way, and after a while they lose their drive to follow Jesus. They don't take the time to know the One who saved them and before long they fall back into the way they'd always been.

Jesus talks about this in His message of the sower of the seed in Mark 4:14-20:

The sower soweth the word. 15 And these are they by the way side, where the word is sown; but when they have heard, Satan cometh immediately, and taketh away the word that was sown in their hearts. 16 And these are they likewise which are sown on stony ground; who, when they have heard the word, immediately receive it with gladness; 17 And have no root in themselves, and so endure but for a time: afterward, when affliction or persecution ariseth for the word's sake, immediately they are offended. 18 And these are they which are sown among thorns; such as hear the word, 19 And the cares of this world, and the deceitfulness of riches, and the lusts of other things entering in, choke the word, and it becometh unfruitful. 20 And these are they which are sown on good ground; such as hear the word, and receive it, and bring forth fruit, some thirtyfold, some sixty, and some an hundred.

When we heard the truth for the first time and it actually became a reality to us, God gave us enough faith at that precise moment to believe it. It's a "measure of faith"—a gift—that God gives to each of us so that we can come to the cross and accept His salvation. Without this gift, there is no way that any human could ever receive the truth about Him. Jesus died on the cross for everyone, but only those who accept this gift of faith will believe in Him and get saved.

For by grace are ye saved through faith; and that not of yourselves: it is the gift of God.— Ephesians 2:8

This gift of faith, however, is not enough to fill anyone with the faith needed to follow Jesus. It's a "seed" that needs to be planted. Many will receive it when they hear the good news of salvation, but they will not become a Christian—born again—until this good news goes from the mind of reasoning to the heart of believing. The seed needs to be planted in the heart and then it needs to be nourished so it will grow and turn us into a fully developed Christian.

How does this happen? We need to get into a church that preaches only from the scriptures and where we can be surrounded in Godly fellowship. But we also need to study the Bible our self. We need to know in our heart who God is and why He sent Jesus, and what our part is in the family of God. And we'll only know this when we study the scriptures and spend time in prayer with God because His Spirit will turn the words on the pages into revelation in our heart. If we don't follow through with this immediately, the world will quickly steal the good news from our mind and it will never get planted in our heart.

> Study to shew thyself approved unto God, a workman that needeth not to be ashamed, rightly dividing the word of truth.—2 Timothy 2:15

Many new Christians feel that they aren't qualified to read and understand the Bible on their own and that they need to sit under an official teacher who is supposed to know everything. This is not true. If it were true, then there wouldn't be a person on earth who would qualify to teach the Bible because on their own merits they aren't able to understand one thing about God. No one can know the scripture unless God reveals the truth to them through His Holy Spirit. God will make known the truth of the scriptures to anyone who is hungry to know Him.

> But the Comforter, which is the Holy Ghost, whom the Father will send in my name, He shall teach you all things, and bring all things to your remembrance, whatsoever I have said unto you.—John 14:26

> But God hath revealed them unto us by his Spirit: for the Spirit searcheth all things, yea, the deep things of God.—1 Corinthians 2:10

And choosing the right Bible is crucial! All Bibles are not the true Word of God! Many have been altered to appease the different lifestyles, and sadly, many new

Christians don't know the difference and so they tend to get the one that is most commonly read and easiest to understand. But there is only ONE Holy Bible and it's critical that it's the one we study to know the truth.

A good rule of thumb to follow when purchasing a Bible is to read only translated versions. The King James Version (KJV) is the closest one to the original manuscripts, and the New King James Version (NKJV) is the same content only with more modern dialect that replaces, for example, the "thee's" and "thou's" with "you". The words in these Bibles are translated from the original Greek scriptures; they are not re-interpreted by a modern-day theologian or by someone who wants the Bible to read what they want it to read. The original scriptures were not just words written by men, BUT they were God's inspired words. And He wants us all to read the same content—His words and not man's sinful interpretation of them.

> All scripture is given by inspiration of God, and is profitable for doctrine, for reproof, for correction, for instruction in righteousness.— 2 Timothy 3:16

We need to study the Bible to know God. It's great to begin in the New Testament when the Christian world is born, and then read it over and over so we can get it down into our heart. But then it's important to also go back to the Old Testament and read what happened from the beginning that brought the world to the point of needing a Savior. God may appear harsh at times and that's because He hates sin and He's angry with those who chose to live in it and rule by it and hurt the ones who loved Him. But as we read it over and over, we'll begin to see the big picture unfold, and we'll realize that God loves us and that we're part of His world— and this is a good thing.

We are responsible for what we do with that first seed of faith; accept it and act on it, or let it fall away. It is our responsibility to know God and to study His word and to become the Christian that He has called us to be. He gave His life for us and all we have to do is accept it!

> ...work out your own salvation with fear and trembling.—Philippians 2:12

We cannot recharge our faith batteries by following someone else's teaching. We can only grow in the Lord and increase our faith by reading our Bible so we can know Him, and by spending time in prayer and by praising Him for His faithfulness and for His love toward us. Like batteries in a toy, we need to keep our faith charged! And then with a full charge, we will not only know God, but we will be equipped to carry on His great commission.

> But they that wait upon the Lord shall renew their strength; they shall mount up with wings as eagles; they shall run, and not be weary; and they shall walk, and not faint.—Isaiah 40:31

The Beatitudes of Christ

If we are going to be Christians who truly love and serve the Lord, then we must have His character deep inside us. We are the light of the world; we are the ones who are showing Jesus to the world. So we need to make sure that what the world sees in us is Christ and not us alone. We can learn of His character in Matthew 5:3-12:

The Sermon on the Mount: The Beatitudes of Christ:

3 Blessed are the poor in spirit: for theirs is the kingdom of heaven.

4 Blessed are they that mourn: for they shall be comforted.

5 Blessed are the meek: for they shall inherit the earth.

6 Blessed are they which do hunger and thirst after righteousness: for they shall be filled.

7 Blessed are the merciful: for they shall obtain mercy.

8 Blessed are the pure in heart: for they shall see God.

9 Blessed are the peacemakers: for they shall be called the children of God.

10 Blessed are they which are persecuted for righteousness' sake: for theirs is the kingdom of heaven.

11 Blessed are ye, when men shall revile you, and persecute you, and shall say all manner of evil against you falsely, for my sake.

12 Rejoice, and be exceeding glad: for great is
your reward in heaven: for so persecuted they
the prophets which were before you.

Jesus explains how a Christian should behave and
how their natural reactions to situations should bless others.
While we all fall short of this at the beginning of our walk,
we should constantly be making changes for the good as we
study the Bible and seek God's face.

The poor in spirit are those who once didn't know
Jesus, but when they learned about Him they repented of
their sins, gave up their sinful life and became born again in
Christ. They are blessed because now they have Jesus as their
Lord, the Holy Spirit as their guide and eternal life with God
in Heaven as their inheritance.

The ones that mourn are the ones who have a heart
that is heavy with sorrow and that no situation or person can
seem to lift away. But the Holy Spirit inside them will
comfort them and give them a peace that they could not get
anywhere in the world. God's love pours through them like
only a Father's love could, and they experience a peace and a
rest that the world can't understand.

The meek are the people who love the Lord and come
to Him with reverence and respect for Him as their Father,
Lord, and Almighty God. These are the ones who will inherit
eternity with Christ and come back with Him to live on the
earth. It's not for the ones who "name and claim" their
inheritance now, or who chant scriptures, or who raise
themselves up to be equal with God. The "meek" are the
Christians who love the Lord with all their heart, mind, soul
and strength and who love others with the same humility.

The ones who hunger and thirst for righteousness are
the ones who love Jesus and want to know Him. These are

the people who are not concerned with personal financial gain or career objectives, but who love the Lord and who live for the Lord. They know that if they have needs, God will supply them, and if they are sick that God will heal them. So their focus is to serve the Lord above everything else. They believe that the righteousness of Christ is everything and they hunger and thirst to know Him and to be with Him.

The merciful are those who treat others with the same love and patience, kindness and forgiveness, compassion and understanding as Jesus gives to them. They know that Jesus loves them and died for them on the cross while they were still sinners. They know that He doesn't give up on them when they do things wrong and that when they repent He forgives them. So they extend this same mercy and compassion towards others, and they don't judge or condemn, raise themselves up or knock others down. They let Christ live through them and show His mercy towards them.

The pure in heart are those who are washed in the blood of Jesus, have repented of their sins and turned away from their sinful life to follow Jesus with gladness. They are the ones who are covered in His righteousness and who are filled with the Holy Spirit. They are the ones who spend time with God in prayer and worship, and who know Him as their Lord, Savior, King and Friend. They are the ones who know they are part of the family of God and who have a home waiting for them with God in Heaven. And they don't let the sin or corruption of this world steal that joy from them.

The peacemakers are those who talk to people and deal with situations with a peaceful and calming attitude rather than in a harsh or aggressive manner. They don't judge, condemn or criticize others, but rather, they deal with situations and people with understanding, wisdom and compassion. They don't strike back and retaliate when they're called names or when false accusations come against them. They know who they are in Christ and these offenses fall to the wayside. They go out of their way to keep and promote peace among all people at all times.

The persecuted for righteousness' sake are the ones who stand for Christ at any cost and don't back down. Their heart is to serve their Lord and nothing this world does to hurt them will change their directive. They are the ones who are martyred for the Lord because they stand for His truth even when threatened to keep quiet, and they are also the ones who simply live their life to please the Lord in spite of what others think. They are the ones who speak out against sin and who don't allow the negative reactions of the world to change who they are. They are the ones who wear the full armor of God so they can withstand the wiles of the devil. They let embarrassment or pride or worldly status prevent them from preaching the gospel of Christ because they love the Lord and they will preach His gospel at any cost.

The blessings of God in each of our lives make life worth living. We cannot preach the gospel without His character in us, and we cannot be nice to mean people on our own efforts. God is our Heavenly Father. He loves us enough to send Jesus to die for us so that we could be redeemed back to Him. And He's prepared a home for us in Heaven where He waits for us to come. He's given us these precious Beatitudes so that we can know the heart of God and learn to be like Him because when we're like Him, we can see others the way He sees them.

> Finally, be ye all of one mind, having compassion one of another, love as brethren, be pitiful, be courteous: 9 Not rendering evil for evil, or railing for railing: but contrariwise blessing; knowing that ye are thereunto called, that ye should inherit a blessing.—1 Peter 3:8-9

No Thanks to the Blind

One of the most festive seasons of the year is Thanksgiving! It's a time when many people prepare for weeks to engage in a time of family gatherings, great food and appreciation for the good things in life. And yet many people will enter into the celebration with a heart filled with anxiety because the situations in their own lives steal the joy of thanksgiving from them. They feel that they don't have anything to be thankful for and they become blinded to the true things of God. And because they are blinded, they are not able to give God the thanks that He deserves.

The problem that many of us have is that our thoughts and goals are limited to the successes achieved in this world. We compare our lives to those who have mastered financial and material success and we foolishly or unwittingly think that we are inferior because we didn't achieve our own desires and goals. It's the same concept with our health; when we become ill we tend to believe the stories from Hollywood and feel that money does buy health and happiness, and then we get bitter because our healing doesn't seem to come. Our big mistake is that we too often make this world our benchmark, and we become ungrateful because of what we don't have compared to what others do have.

> Lay not up for yourselves treasures upon earth, where moth and rust doth corrupt, and where thieves break through and steal: 20 But lay up for yourselves treasures in heaven, where neither moth nor rust doth corrupt, and where thieves do not break through nor steal: 21 For where your treasure is, there will your heart be also.—Matthew 6:19-21

Everything and everyone that we compare our lives to here on earth is an error that will not only keep us in a state of ingratitude, but will unknowingly to us keep us giving glory to the devil for the bad things he's doing. No wonder we can't be grateful! We need to keep our eyes on Jesus and realize that we live "in" this world—the devil's world—but we don't belong "to" this world. Jesus is OUR king and He alone is the One who will give us the victory through the trials of our life. And He alone is the One who deserves ALL of our praises and thanksgiving whether we see the victories in our life or not!

When we can realize that Jesus gave His life to save ours so that sin could no longer judge us, so that His Spirit could live in us, and so that we could have a perfect relationship with our Heavenly Father, then we will realize that anything we accomplish in this world is for nothing. When we get to Heaven, God isn't going to give us a crown filled with jewels that reflect the money we earned here, or the rich house we built to live in, or the status we set up for ourselves that allowed us to publically donate thousands or millions of dollars to help the underprivileged.

> Take heed that ye do not your alms before men, to be seen of them: otherwise ye have no reward of your Father which is in Heaven.— Matthew 6:1

When we can see with our heart that Jesus is our Savior, our King, our Deliverer, our Healer and our God, and that He rewards those who diligently seek after Him and help others to find Him, then we will realize that God has given us something far greater than this world can ever offer. We will be truly thankful to God for our life, for our blessings and even for our sorrows because we will know that He can and will turn them all around for our good.

> And we know that all things work together for good to them that love God, to them who are

the called according to his purpose.—Romans 8:28

When we give thanks to God simply because He loves us, then we will feel a joy in our heart that no earthly possession could ever give us. When we can praise Him because He took our sins upon Himself at the cross so that we could be saved from the wrath and judgment that is about to come upon this earth, then our hearts will rejoice. When we can realize that sickness and sin belong to the same curse and that on the cross He removed all sickness from us, then we will shout endless praises to His name. Yes, we will endure trials here on earth and we will suffer because of them, but when we remember that Jesus has already overcome every tribulation that could be set before us, and that He will go through them all with us, then our heart pours out endless praises to our God.

> These things I have spoken unto you, that in me ye might have peace. In the world ye shall have tribulation: but be of good cheer; I have overcome the world.—John 16:33

We can't come to God with a grateful heart if we are secretly not happy because of things we don't have, or because of trials that we are enduring that we hate, or because we or a loved one are ill and the world's prognosis is dim. We need to rise up above this negative mindset and thank God anyway because He is greater than the world! He is greater than any problem we have! He has overcome the world! And He will help us to overcome it, too.

> Ye are of God, little children, and have overcome them: because greater is He that is in you, than he that is in the world.—1 John 4:4

Jesus took away all of our sin and everything that goes with it including lack of material needs, sickness and sadness. We need to look beyond ourselves and see the cross. We need to realize that God has provided it all for us and that we need to believe it and thank Him for it. His word is true and He is faithful to His word. If He said it, then it is so. Believe it! Accept it! Expect it! And thank Him for it even if we haven't received it yet!

> For we walk by faith, not by sight.—2 Corinthians 5:7

We cannot allow ourselves to be blind in the heart or we will miss God's plan for our life. We are surrounded with sin and sickness, but we don't have to be part of it. Our heart and our eyes should be focused on Jesus alone. He is coming soon to end the evil in this world. And He's coming to get us so we can be with Him forever. And He's going to give us not only a Crown of Life, but a Crown of Rejoicing, and this is the reward we receive for reaching out to others with the gospel of Jesus. What joy it will be when we can lay down our crowns at His throne! We have so much to look forward to and so much to be thankful for.

> For what is our hope, or joy, or crown of rejoicing? Are not even ye in the presence of our Lord Jesus Christ at his coming?—1 Thessalonians 2:19

Our blessings of material wealth and a good life here on earth are just that—blessings from God. And truly, we are grateful to Him for them all. But they are not our accomplishments; they are His blessings to us. We are grateful that He saved us and that He cares for us.

We can never thank God enough for His faithfulness. And there is no greater way to show God how much we love

Him and thank Him for His love toward us than to share His love and truth with others. When Jesus was talking to Peter, He told him that there was no greater way to express his love to God than to preach the gospel. And Peter is our example and someone who we can learn from when we want to express our thanks to God.

> He saith unto him the third time, 'Simon, son of Jonas, lovest thou me?' Peter was grieved because He said unto him the third time, 'Lovest thou me?' And he said unto Him, 'Lord, thou knowest all things; thou knowest that I love thee.' Jesus saith unto him, 'Feed my sheep.'—John 21:17

Choosing What Scriptures to Accept

Many so-called Christians have no idea who God is or what the Bible is about because they pick through the scriptures and select only the ones that best suit their desires or lifestyles. They have no interest in knowing God; just in receiving from Him. They have no intention of changing and they expect God to accept them as they are. They pick what scriptures suit them and ignore the rest. But this attitude is dangerous because the scriptures were given by God so that believers could study them *all* and know Him! Every word in the Bible compromises a part of God's plan for us and we cannot know Him or the truth when we pick what scriptures we will accept.

Many new age believers say that the Bible is filled with errors because it's written by men. It also claims that reading the Bible is not an essential part of a believer's life because it's unreliable, and that believers should be led by the spirit that's in their heart and not be dependent upon a book. So, they pick what they want to believe and debate the rest.

The original Holy Scriptures were inspired by God. They were written by devoted men over a period of many years as God instructed them through His Holy Spirit. This is why the entire collection of scriptures that we call the Bible is totally of God and not of men. These transcribers, known as scribes, were very devoted to God and to transcribing the scriptures with total accuracy.

All scripture is given by inspiration of God, and is profitable for doctrine, for reproof, for correction, for instruction in righteousness.—
2 Timothy 3:16

However, not all bibles are equal! Not all bibles are the inspired word of God because there are some that have been revised by people who have even deleted some verses just to suit modern-day lifestyles. And yes, these are filled with errors. So, when we're looking to purchase a bible, we need to find one that is a true translation and that replicates the original manuscripts such as the King James Version [KJV] or the New King James Version [NKJV]. Yes, there may be a typo here or there, or a punctuation slip, but for the most part these bibles are as closely translated from the original scriptures as any bible can be, and so they remain to be called the Holy Bible.

Some of the bibles out there cater specifically to false doctrines and some of these include the Jehovah Witness Bible, the Mormon Bible and the Catholic Bible. Most Christians will avoid these versions because they know they are not authentic translations of the original scriptures, and they know that the merits of these books are in line with the false doctrines being taught.

However, there are other bibles that are discreetly disguised as authentic and can deceive Christians who don't know what to look for. In fact, many teachers and pastors will use one of these versions to easily explain the scriptures and teach their lessons. The two most common versions to avoid are the New International Version (NIV) and the English Standard Version (ESV). These are widely accepted because the changes in wording and meanings are just enough to avoid conviction and the need for repentance. And this is what far too many "Christians" are looking for.

Neither of these bibles are "translations" of the original scriptures. They are "interpretations" of the scriptures; they have been rewritten by humans to be acceptable to people, and they are not intended to convict or to teach the truth. The danger is that man is interpreting what he thinks it means—or what he wants it to mean—and not what God instructed the original authors to write. God has not changed and neither has His scriptures changed. And believers need to know the difference!

> Jesus Christ, the same yesterday, today, and forever.—Hebrews 13:8

The first scribes spent their lives translating the scriptures and writing the manuscripts, and they did this prayerfully and fearfully as they would not allow one word to be misinterpreted or misquoted. They gave their lives to protect the scriptures. However, modern day scribes have a different mindset and they feel justified to change the words. In their mind, they are simply writing it so we can better understand it, but sadly, too often the content is reworded in such a way that the meaning is changed. So we really do need to know that the bible we study is a real translation of the original scriptures given by God.

With the market being flooded with so many versions of bibles, we can see why the new age religion says that the bible isn't consistent and that it's loaded with errors and that God changes over time. They don't realize that these "modified" versions are not the Holy Bible! And so it's no wonder that they pick and choose what verses they'll believe.

The Holy Bible is a collection of all of the scriptures that God gave to trusted men to write out for our benefit. The history of the Jewish people and of the church is clearly set out on its pages, and the return of Christ is prominently presented to us in both Old and New Testaments. We need to know all of these things if we are going to know God and know what His plan is for us.

Nothing new is being given out today by God—no new revelation and no new laws. Jesus accomplished it all at the cross when He said, "It is finished"—John 19:30. There is nothing more for Him to do except to return to earth as King, fight His final battle against the devil and establish His throne here. He shared His thoughts and His plans with His disciples who became His apostles. And the message they preached was what Jesus told them to preach, and it's the same message that's in the Holy Bible and that we are to preach today. We are not allowed to modify or change the scriptures in any way! We do not have that authority!

> But I certify you, Brethren, that the gospel which was preached of me is not after man. 12 For I neither received it of man, neither was I taught it, but by the revelation of Jesus Christ.—Galatians 1:11-12

> But though we or an angel from heaven preach any other gospel unto you than that which we have preached unto you, let him be accursed. 9 As we said before, so say I now again, if any man preach any other gospel unto you than that ye have received, let him be accursed.—Galatians 1:8-9

The Holy Bible is truly inerrant—without error—and we are told to study it prayerfully and to accept and believe it because it's God revelation to us. But this is just too much commitment for some people because it also means change; it means coming away from their sinful lifestyle that they are comfortable in and not willing to give up. It's easier for some people to serve a god that they make up in their mind to be the God of Heaven, than it is to have to repent of their sins, accept Jesus as their personal Lord and Savior and follow Him—and change. They foolishly feel that what they're doing is good enough.

We can't let convenience or pride or a sinful lifestyle keep us from knowing the truth. Contrary to false teaching, the life we have on this earth is the only time we'll have to accept Jesus' forgiveness for our sins. We don't get to decide when we stand before Him at the Great White Throne. The Bible tells us in Romans 14:11 that every knee will bow and every tongue will confess that Jesus is Lord, and every one of those people who chose to believe a false doctrine and pick what scriptures they'd believe instead of repenting for their sins, will certainly know it's Him when they stand before Him—but it will be too late to repent then.

We must accept the Holy Bible in its entirety as God's word for us and we must turn from our sin and follow Him now! And one day we'll all stand before Him and if our name isn't written in the Book of Life—if we did not accept Jesus as our Savior and follow Him—then we will face His judgment. Will He find your name written in that Book?

> But continue thou in the things which thou hast learned and hast been assured of, knowing of whom thou hast learned them; 15 And that from a child thou hast known the holy scriptures, which are able to make thee wise unto salvation through faith which is in Christ Jesus.—2 Timothy 3:14-15

Stop the Backbiting

Sometimes when we spend a lot of time with other Christians the conversation somehow drifts into gossip. With good intentions, we set out to have a great fellowship, but we end up talking and criticizing others, and some of us even begin judging others according to what we think we know about their actions. And if we go online and join some of the social media Christian discussions, we'll see very clearly how some proclaimed Christians have no qualms about publically criticizing and judging others. This is not what God wants for His children. He wants us to love each other and to stop the backbiting!

None of us are perfect. We all once lived in sin and we all had to be washed in the blood of Jesus. And we still continue to fall into acts of sin now and then and need to come to Jesus and ask for forgiveness. Most of us are not of the Jewish lineage and have been adopted into God's family. We have different backgrounds and come from various walks of life, and we all have situations to overcome that may be very unlike those of our brethren. When we can focus on the scriptures and spend time in prayer and in praising the Lord, we'll realize how wrong it is to waste time talking about things that don't glorify God.

> For all have sinned, and come short of the glory of God.—Romans 3:23

God told us in Matthew 7 that we are not to judge each other, but that we are to love each other and pray for each other—Colossians 3:16. And many Christians get this confused with what Paul said when he told us to judge the doctrines that are being preached, as well as those who preach them. Our spiritual walk depends on following only God's gospel, so we need to know that what we're being taught is truth. We cannot just accept it as truth; we must always compare what is being taught to what the scriptures say. And when we know that the leader is not teaching the truth, we're told to speak to them and try and correct them, and to even warn others to not listen to them if they won't change. Through searching the scriptures we can know whether or not what is being preached is from God and judge it accordingly.

> These were more noble than those in Thessalonica, in that they received the word with all readiness of mind, and searched the scriptures daily, whether those things were so.—Acts 17:11

Jesus has warned us to beware of the false leaders and since many new Christians don't know the scriptures well enough to discern what they are teaching, it's good that mature Christians point these false preachers out to them for their own safety. But it shouldn't become a goal in life to search out these individuals so we can regularly declare who they are and judge them. It's not the Christian's responsibility to bring them down because that is the authority and responsibility of the Lord. He will judge them and send them to their final destination.

Our objective in life is to preach the good news so people can be saved, and our love for God is shared as we love each other and encourage each other to follow Jesus. This is sharing God's love; this is doing His will. But when we continually talk badly about someone and discuss their faults and their wrong doings, we are giving Satan the glory, and nowhere in the Bible does God tell us to do this.

> For, brethren, ye have been called unto liberty; only use not liberty for an occasion to the flesh, but by love serve one another.— Galatians 5:13

> Seeing ye have purified your souls in obeying
> the truth through the Spirit unto unfeigned
> love of the brethren, see that ye love one
> another with a pure heart fervently: 23 Being
> born again, not of corruptible seed, but of
> incorruptible, by the word of God, which
> liveth and abideth for ever.—1 Peter 1:22-23

Jesus did not say to condemn and criticize those who
are weak in Christ or those who are not exactly where we are
on the path to Heaven. He said to preach the gospel, love the
brethren, feed the hungry and pray for one another. When
Jesus walked the earth He constantly taught His disciples
about God and Heaven, and He was their example then and
He is our example today of what God, our Heavenly Father,
expects from us.

> Jesus said unto him, 'Thou shalt love the Lord
> thy God with all thy heart, and with all thy
> soul, and with all thy mind. 38 This is the first
> and great commandment. 39 And the second
> is like unto it, Thou shalt love thy neighbour
> as thyself.'—Matthew 22:37-39

> We know that we have passed from death
> unto life, because we love the brethren. He
> that loveth not his brother abideth in death.—
> 1 John 3:14

Some will argue that we can judge others because
Jesus corrected and even criticized the Pharisees and the
Sadducees. And it's true that He did, but only when they
confronted Him. He did not His spend time searching them
out and then going to where they were to criticize and
condemn them. It was when they came to Him and tried to
trick Him and tried to prove Him to be a false prophet that
He rebuked them. If you read the four gospels [Matthew,

Mark, Luke and John] you'll see what Jesus preached and how He addressed those who came against Him.

Our commission from Jesus is to preach the gospel and to love one another, and that doesn't mean criticizing and judging our brethren all the time. We need to be witnesses for God of His love and His grace, of His mercy and His forgiveness, of His strength and His power. And what kind of a witness are we to the world when they see that there is often more animosity between Christians than there is amongst the people of the world?

If it's necessary to correct one of our brethren and we aren't able to do it because we live too far away or because they won't see us, then we should pray for them. God tells us clearly in James 5:16 that we should pray fervently for our brothers and sisters. We read in John 8:7 that when a group of men brought the adulterous woman to Jesus, even He did not condemn her. Instead, He told the accusers, "He that is without sin among you, let him first cast a stone at her." Jesus knew that these people were learned in the scriptures and so He used the scriptures to throw the condemnation back at them, and in shame and conviction they all left her.

Let's not become like the Pharisees and spend our time exalting ourselves through our acts of tearing down others. Let's be humble before God and serve Him with a pure heart and not with one that's filled with judgment toward our brothers and sisters in Christ. We won't earn Brownie points by showing off how many of our brethren we can judge; instead we will subject ourselves to become judged by God.

> For whosoever exalteth himself shall be abased; and he that humbleth himself shall be exalted.—Luke 14:11

When we criticize and gossip about our brothers and sisters, no matter how wrong they may be about some issues, we hurt God. We are all His children and when we fight it hurts Him because He loves all of us equally. He knows that some of us are falling off the path and He knows that others are doing things they shouldn't, but He loves us all anyway. And He expects us to step in and help those who need help, and not to judge and mock them.

So instead of criticizing, we need to spend time in prayer for them and we need to love them with the love of God in spite of how they are acting. It's not our place to judge them. It's our responsibility to be obedient to God's Commission and to share the gospel and His love with others—especially with other Christians regardless of how weak they are. There's no greater way to show gratitude for God's grace toward us than to put judgment aside and let our passion to our own brothers and sisters in Chris be love, just as He loves us.

> Beloved, let us love one another: for love is of God; and every one that loveth is born of God, and knoweth God. 8 He that loveth not knoweth not God; for God is love. 9 In this was manifested the love of God toward us, because that God sent His only begotten Son into the world, that we might live through Him. 10 Herein is love, not that we loved God, but that He loved us, and sent His Son to be the propitiation for our sins. 11 Beloved, if God so loved us, we ought also to love one another.—1 John 4:7-11

Christians: Forgiven not Perfect!

As we travel forward in our Christian walk, we realize that not everyone we meet along the path is at the same place we are in our personal relationship with God. Some will be brand new Christians and others will have a mature walk with God. Some were once back-sliders and are now back onto the path while others still need to be prompted to get back on. There are those who are abundant in love and radiate in peace while others are still focused on material gain and self assurance. Some have a shallow understanding of the scriptures while others have a deep revelation of the truth. We've come from various backgrounds, been brought through different circumstances, and have our individual mountains to climb, but we all have one thing in common. We are all sinners saved by grace. Not one of us is perfect, but we are all forgiven!

We all once belonged to the world and were under the law of God and ready to be judged by the law because we had all violated God's laws at one time or another. Even if we broke only one law in the tiniest way, that sin separated us from God and subjected us to His judgment by the law. But now we are no longer under the law because of Jesus' shed blood. He became the ultimate sacrifice and our atonement before God for all of our sins, and when we personally and individually repent for our sins and accept Jesus as our Lord and Savior then we will be saved from the punishment that will come to all who still have sin in them. Now we are not under the law but under grace. So when we stand before God on Judgment Day, He won't judge us according to the law because we are not under that ruling. We are under the blood of Jesus and we have been forgiven for all the laws of God that we broke—for all of our sins.

Ronnie Dauber

> If we say that we have no sin, we deceive
> ourselves, and the truth is not in us.—1 John
> 1:8

We are forgiven! We have been redeemed back to
God, and every sin we ever committed before we accepted
Jesus as our Lord and Savior was forgiven. The record has
been washed clean and God doesn't see it anymore. We now
live under grace. We are no longer under the law and sin can
no longer hurt us.

> But when the fullness of the time was come,
> God sent forth his Son, made of a woman,
> made under the law, 5 To redeem them that
> were under the law, that we might receive the
> adoption of sons.—Galatians 4:4-5

Without God's forgiveness we would still have sin in
us, and so when we commit even one sin, one felony or
offence, a single transgression against the law, we commit
that sin against God. He gave us the law through Moses and
it's known as The Ten Commandments that can read in
Exodus 20:3-17. The Bible says in Romans 3:23 that "we
have all sinned and fall short of the glory of God," so we
know that it is impossible to live without sinning. This means
that every person has sinned and, therefore, would be
responsible to suffer the punishment for their sins if Jesus
had not saved us.

If it were possible for any person to live one hundred
percent according to this law and never once waiver even in
the slightest bit throughout their entire life, they would still
need a Savior because they were born with a sinful heart.
And that heart has to be removed through salvation and
replaced with a new one, and then God's Spirit lives within
us. This is what we call being born again—John 3:3.

46

God loves us with a love so great that few people can really comprehend it. It grieved God terribly to have been separated from Adam and Eve because of sin. It was His plan to take that sin away from them and from every person ever born because He knew the punishment of sin. He made the world; He made the law and it stands.

> For the wages of sin is death; but the gift of
> God is eternal life through Jesus Christ our
> Lord.—Romans 6:23

The "death" spoken of here doesn't refer to the death of our earthly bodies, but of the second death that will come to those people on Judgment Day when they stand before Christ and still have sin in them. The punishment will come to them because of this sin and it will be a complete separation from God forever.

> Then said the king to the servants, 'Bind him
> hand and foot, and take him away, and cast
> him into outer darkness'; there shall be
> weeping and gnashing of teeth.—Matthew
> 22:13

Jesus is the only person ever to have lived a totally sinless life. He was born of a woman, but His father was God, and God is Holy; therefore, Jesus is Holy. Since He was not born of a man, He did not inherit the sin of Adam as the rest of the human race did. He had God's Spirit in Him.

> For we have not an high priest which cannot
> be touched with the feeling of our infirmities;
> but was in all points tempted like as we are,
> yet without sin.—Hebrews 4:15

Jesus became the propitiation for our sins. He was the Lamb of God who died on the cross and took upon Himself all of our sins so that those who accept His sacrifice would be

47

forgiven and would live under the grace of God. This means that if during our Christian lives here on earth we do something that we know is wrong, we can come to God immediately and ask Him to forgive us, and He'll not only forgive us, but He'll erase it from our record forever.

> For God so loved the world that He gave His only begotten Son, that whoever believes in Him should not perish but have everlasting life.—John 3:16

We are forgiven! We live under the grace of God and as we grow and pray and study the Bible and worship the Lord, we become more and more like Him through the Holy Spirit who lives in us. But every Christian won't be like us. We shouldn't judge them or put them down, but instead we need to show the love and grace of God toward them. We need to pray for them and teach them at their level so they can see God from where they are and grow into a wonderful relationship with Him.

> Let the word of Christ dwell in you richly in all wisdom, teaching and admonishing one another in psalms and hymns and spiritual songs, singing with grace in your hearts to the Lord.— Colossians 3:16

The Christian life is wonderful when we see others through the eyes of Jesus and not through our own ideals. There are many people around us who aren't Christians, but who watch us and who secretly would like to know God. We need to treat all people with love and compassion, using only scripture as a benchmark and God's love and grace in our character toward them so they can see Him. But we also need to tell those who still live in sin about His judgment so they'll know why they need to repent.

The difference between Christians and people of the world is that we are forgiven! The people of the world have not been forgiven for their sins and they still live under the law and will be judged by the law one day. Christians have been washed clean of their sins through the saving blood of Jesus at the cross. Yes, we all still sin on occasion, but we live under grace and can repent and are forgiven; a privilege that comes to those who accept Jesus as their Lord and Savior.

> Blessed is he whose transgression is forgiven,
> whose sin is covered.—Psalm 32:1

Close Your Eyes and See

There is so much deception all around us in the world today that it's almost impossible to know what is true. Our benchmark has become one of false promises and forged hopes, and many of us have foolishly accepted these pretences because they're easy and convenient. Lies and deception will lead to inevitable destruction and will come to all those who choose to follow it rather than the truth. But there's still time to close your eyes and see the truth.

Many people want everything in life and they want to get it the easiest way! So they follow a prosperity doctrine that says Jesus died on the cross and that gives them a bit of security, but the emphasis is not on salvation and preaching the gospel. It's on God's purpose to make life happy and prosperous here on earth with a guaranteed home in Heaven when we leave. They don't know Jesus because repentance isn't taught and they've never been born again—(John 3:1-3). They don't see Christ as their Savior; only as someone who will give them whatever they want now. They think life is good because they attend a church or because they tithe, but they don't read their Bible or spend time in prayer and they have no idea who Jesus really is. Nor do they care.

> This know also, that in the last days perilous times shall come. 2 For men shall be lovers of their own selves, covetous, boasters, proud, blasphemers, disobedient to parents, unthankful, unholy, 3 Without natural affection, trucebreakers, false accusers, incontinent, fierce, despisers of those that are good, 4 Traitors, heady, high-minded, lovers of pleasures more than lovers of God; 5 Having a form of godliness, but denying the power thereof: from such turn away.—2 Timothy 3:1-5 NKJV

While the prosperity message continues to grow, the world is looking for one religion—one that will make us all brethren and one where we don't need to come to Jesus and repent for our sins or change our lifestyle or even read the Bible. The deception of this heresy is it teaches that God loves us all just as we are. It says that the Bible contains errors; that it was written by men and under their own opinion; that there is no such thing as hell or judgment for people. And so anyone who believes this thinks that life is what you make it and that Heaven is for everyone. They only see God as love, but He's also a God of justice and judgment, and this is the part that they won't accept.

> Know ye not that the unrighteous shall not inherit the kingdom of God? Be not deceived: neither fornicators, nor idolaters, nor adulterers, nor effeminate, nor abusers of themselves with mankind, 10 Nor thieves, nor covetous, nor drunkards, nor revilers, nor extortioners, shall inherit the kingdom of God.—1 Corinthians 6:9-10

People need to close their eyes to this deception and stop looking at themselves in the mirror and gloating over how great they are because of their faith. It's time to become humble and realize how sinful they are and how they need to repent and accept Jesus as their Lord so that they can live life the way God intended.

We are not the reason God lives; we live because of God! His promises were to the Jewish people, but we have been given the privilege of being grafted into God's family—(Romans 11:17) and to receive His promises. We need to dig deep into our soul and if Jesus isn't in the centre of our being, then we need to repent! We need to search for the truth and find it and stop delving into the sins of a heretic religion.

> And ye shall know the truth, and the truth
> shall make you free.—John 8:32

The Bible is our only source of truth because it is the inspired word of God. BUT we need to read it prayerfully to know God and to absorb the message that He is giving to us. We can't cherry pick what scriptures suit us because in the end, it really doesn't matter; what God has said stands! We'll all bow to Jesus because He is our King, and we either do it now from a loving heart or on Judgment out of fear and reverence. We have to realize that what we choose to believe doesn't change the truth. God cannot be seen in different ways; He is the same yesterday, today and forever—Hebrews 13:8. We either accept the truth and live in it now, or deny it and are judged by it later.

> For it is written, 'As I live', saith the Lord,
> 'every knee shall bow to me, and every
> tongue shall confess to God'.—Romans 14:11

Only a fool would assume that they're going to Heaven and say that God is all love and doesn't judge or that people won't go to hell. A wise person would not assume anything, but would search for the truth in the scriptures and know it! The Bible is the only source of truth, and contrary to those who don't know it, the Bible doesn't give conflicting messages, nor does it speak contrary about anything.

God gave His Son as the ultimate sacrifice, the Lamb of God, to die brutally on the cross and take on the punishment for our sins, and those who don't want to accept that are going to pay the price of their sins themselves. Romans 6:23 says, "The wages of sin is death." God does love us that much or else He wouldn't have sent Jesus to be our Savior, but He also hates sin that much and He's made it clear that sin will be punished. Those who don't accept God's gift of life and who either blatantly engage in sin or who are deceived into it, will be punished and that punishment is death. But it's not the physical death of leaving the earthly body; it's the second death—an eternal separation from God.

This gift of life is free for everyone. God is not bias on who He'll accept or who He'll bless on earth. He gave His life for everyone! But we must choose to accept it, and when we do He will become our greatest love. Yet sadly, people don't search the scriptures to know the truth and they let false doctrines delude them into thinking that God loves them just as they are and that they're going to Heaven. The truth is that they still belong to this world and to the devil. And yes, they will still be judged on Judgment Day because the sins of this world are still in them.

> For God so loved the world that He gave His only begotten Son, that whoever believes in Him should not perish but have everlasting life. 17 For God did not send His Son into the world to condemn the world, but that the world through Him might be saved.—John 3:16-17

Don't be deceived! God does not change His truth to suit this modern world; it will line up with God's laws or be judged by them. Hell is real and God does not take pleasure in anyone going there—that's why He died on the cross and made salvation available to everyone. Yet, many will find themselves in that line leading to a hell that they foolishly said didn't exist, and it will be too late then to repent.

When we seek the truth, we'll see Jesus as our King, and we'll worship God because we love Him. And He will care for us and love us unconditionally, and when we leave earth He will welcome us Home to live with Him forever.

Close your eyes and see the truth! It will set you free!

Let not your heart be troubled: ye believe in God, believe also in me. 2 In my Father's house are many mansions: if it were not so, I would have told you. I go to prepare a place for you. 3 And if I go and prepare a place for you, I will come again, and receive you unto myself; that where I am, there ye may be also.—John 14:1-3

It's Time to Come out of the Closet

Most of us are familiar with the expression, "coming out of the closet". We relate it to people who once felt ashamed of their "sinful" lifestyle, but who have come public since society no longer views it as sin. But this closet also hides many Christians who appear to be ashamed to speak up because society doesn't want to hear it. They hide in that proverbial closet and have more fear of what society thinks than of what God says. It's time to come out of that closet and speak up so we can be the voice of God in this world.

Years ago, even unbelievers had a reverence for the Ten Commandments and a fear of God for breaking them. But things have changed dramatically over the years! Some things that God called sin are no longer deemed as sin according to our earthly laws. Those who proclaim to be "gay" no longer hide, but rather, flaunt their legally acclaimed lifestyle and no one dares to challenge it. People murder unborn babies by the hundreds of thousands and feel no remorse because, after all, they aren't legally people, just a "fetuses".

Those who commit these sins are no longer ashamed. They mock God and prefer to live their lives apart from Him. They feel that this world has finally evolved into equality for all—and the closet Christians don't oppose it! They just go along with it.

> This know also, that in the last days perilous times shall come. 2 For men shall be lovers of their own selves, covetous, boasters, proud, blasphemers, disobedient to parents, unthankful, unholy, 3 Without natural affection, trucebreakers, false accusers, incontinent, fierce, despisers of those that are good, 4 Traitors, heady, high-minded, lovers

of pleasures more than lovers of God; 5 Having a form of godliness, but denying the power thereof: from such turn away.—2 Timothy 3:1-5

But God does not change; He is the same yesterday, today and forever—Hebrews 13:8. What He called sin in the Old Testament was still sin in the New Testament and is still sin today! And He is going to judge these sins one day by the law that He gave to all of us through Moses, and all those who laugh at them now will certainly not laugh then. And all those who call themselves Christians but who don't defend God's laws, and who don't speak up and call sin what it is— "sin", will have to account for their negative actions one day! We are either "for" God or we're not, but we cannot serve two masters—Matthew 6:24. And neither can we be willing to accept the blessings of being a Christian and at the same time be ashamed to speak out as God's ambassadors.

But whoever denies Me before men, him I will also deny before My Father who is in Heaven.—Matthew 10:33

We should not be ashamed of the gospel of Jesus. He was not ashamed when He left His glorious throne in Heaven to become a lowly earthly man who didn't even own a bed in this world. He wasn't ashamed when He took the brutal beatings and was stripped of His clothing and hung publicly on the cross to die for us. He was not ashamed to die for all of mankind even though most would not receive Him.

Jesus is a King and yet He humbled Himself and became the Lamb of God for our sake, just as it was prophesied in Isaiah 5. When we read of some of the horrific sins that some people have committed, we are sickened and wish the worst of punishment for them. Yet, Christ died for them anyway so they could have the opportunity to repent and be forgiven for those sins. Psalm 45:7 says that God hates sin, and yet on the cross He became sin for us.

> For God so loved the world, that He gave His only begotten Son, that whosoever believeth in Him should not perish, but have everlasting life. 17 For God sent not His Son into the world to condemn the world; but that the world through Him might be saved.—John 3:16-17

We should not hide the truth from the world. God filled us with His light—with His Spirit—so that we could be witnesses of His love, His grace and His power and so we could warn people of the judgment to come. How else will people of the world know what God thinks except through us? The world is in darkness, controlled by a devil who wants to steal from us, kill us and destroy us—John 10:10. We are the light of the world and if we don't let our light shine, then the world will continue to live in darkness.

> That ye may be blameless and harmless, the sons of God, without rebuke, in the midst of a crooked and perverse nation, among whom ye shine as lights in the world.—Philippians 2:15

> Let your light so shine before men, that they may see your good works, and glorify your Father which is in heaven.—Matthew 5:16

Christians are also referred to as the salt of the earth. What does this mean? Salt is the spice we put on food, not only preserve to it, but to make it taste better—but it also makes us thirsty. And this is a good thing because we need to drink when we eat to help digest the food. It's the same concept when Christians are witnesses for Christ. The people see us and hear us and they get thirsty for God. They want to preserve their lives in eternity, and only God can quench that thirst with salvation. But we need to be that salt and create that thirst.

> Ye are the salt of the earth: but if the salt has lost his savour, wherewith shall it be salted? It is thenceforth good for nothing, but to be cast out, and to be trodden under foot of men.— Matthew 5:13

When Christians lose their seasoning of salt—their zest—they blend in with the rest of the world and don't appear any different. If we don't preach the truth and don't point out sin as being sin according to God's law, then how will anyone become thirsty for the truth? If people think that it's okay to live in sin, they will never come to the cross and will never get saved. We need to be bold and not be ashamed to speak out. We can't go with the flow when it comes to sin. We need to speak out and call it what it is—sin!

We won't make a lot of friends; in fact, we may lose some. Christians may even shy away from us because we are too bold and they'd rather not stir the water; they'd prefer to just let people live their lives their own way. Others will think that we are "judging" the brethren when we speak out against sin. But we are not judging anyone; we're a voice crying out for people to recognize sin and turn away from it. So there will be times when we won't be well received, but that's okay, because Jesus wasn't, either.

> And ye shall be hated of all men for My name's sake: but he that endureth to the end shall be saved.—Matthew 10:22

God does love all of us, but He does not accept any of us on our own merits because of the sin that's in us. This is why God sent Jesus to us, to die on the cross and take those sins away. We need to be a witness for God in our own lives because people of the world will only see God through us. If we stay quiet and hide the truth they will never know the truth. But if we speak up, call sin what it is, and encourage people to repent and accept Jesus, then we will be the disciples God has called us to be.

Let's not disobey God. Let's not hide His truth from the world. Let's show how much we love God by sharing His love, truth and salvation message with others. Let's speak out and declare Jesus to all the nations! Time is running out. The onus is on us to get the truth out there so people can get it! We are God's disciples and His Spirit goes with us. But we cannot spread His gospel if we stay hidden in the closet.

> For I am not ashamed of the gospel of Christ:
> for it is the power of God unto salvation to
> everyone that believeth; to the Jew first, and
> also to the Greek.—Romans 1:16

Itching Ears

Years ago we knew who the "Christians" were because their values and the way they dressed revealed a reverence for God. The church bells would ring out on Sunday mornings and everybody knew that it was the Lord's Day, even those who didn't really believe in God. But gradually, the Christians' desire to serve God alone got blended with their own ideals of what they wanted from God. And now today we have dozens of churches with different interpretations of the scriptures and of God's laws, and "Christians" are able to pick which one caters to their personal needs. Where our heart used to search to find God in church, now many are led by their itching ears to find the church that pleases them, and doesn't force them to have to change who they are.

People seem to forget—or perhaps they just simply don't want to accept—that Christianity is not about them. It's not about God changing His ways to make our lives more convenient to this sinful nature; Christianity is about Christ! It's about accepting what God has done so that we can live apart from the sin—not in it! God created the world in His perfection and then sin infiltrated His creation. But sin cannot exist in God's presence, which is why He had to exile Adam and Eve from the "perfect" Garden of Eden [Genesis 3:24]. And we are their descendents and we can't be in God's presence, either. We can't come to Him or even pray to Him in our sinful state because His Holiness would destroy us before we could get the first word out.

We know from Romans 6:23 that the wages of sin is death—death because anyone or anything that has sin in them cannot live in God's presence. But God loves the people He's created and He does not want anyone to be separated from Him—not while we live on this earth and definitely not when we leave this world to go into eternity. God wants us all to be saved from the judgment that will come upon this earth in the very near future, and it's a judgment that brings the sentence of death upon all of those who are found with sin in them.

> For God so loved the world, that He gave His only begotten Son, that whosoever believeth in Him should not perish, but have everlasting life. 17 For God sent not His Son into the world to condemn the world; but that the world through Him might be saved.—John 3:16-17

What we need to understand is that GOD DOES NOT CHANGE! Not even a little bit. The laws that He gave to Moses in the Old Testament still stand firm today. They do not and cannot waiver, and while we live in this world we are expected to obey these laws. We know that in this world when we break any law, we are charged and usually punished. We are given an opportunity in court to have everything clearly revealed so that the judge knows what law or laws we broke (and these are all based on the Mosaic Laws) and then we are judged, sentenced and punished accordingly. The law that we broke is the one that gets us. It's the benchmark by which we are judged and punished.

And so it is on the great Judgment Day to come. We will be judged by each law that we have broken. There isn't a single person on earth who has not broken at least one of these—it doesn't matter how great or small that break is; if we broke it then we are guilty of sin and we WILL be judged, and the wages of sin is death—Romans 6:23.

When Peter told Jesus that he knew Jesus was the Son of God, Jesus told him that this revelation, this truth, would be the rock or the gospel for all believers to follow. So if we say that we follow Jesus, that we are a Christian, then we must accept the full gospel of Christ and follow Him alone—and we must obey it. Our lives must be true to the salvation that Jesus gave on the cross and our testimony must be a witness of this fact in the way we live.

> And I say also unto thee, 'That thou art Peter, and upon this rock I will build my church; and the gates of hell shall not prevail against it.'—Matthew 16:18

Therefore, the gospel or the doctrine that we follow as Christians is the gospel of Jesus only! There is no diversion from this truth. We either, accept and believe this truth or continue to live in sin and face judgment. But unfortunately, there are false preachers all around us who will try to convince us that God has changed and that we were all forgiven at the cross so we can continue to live in sin and enjoy life however we (sinfully) please. These false teachers are wolves in sheep's clothing and their message will kill you! Literally!

Any denomination that changes a single word of the scriptures is not one that is following Christ. The Bible is all about Christ! The Old Testament is not just a history book, but it's a book of prophesy that prepares us for the birth of Christ in the New Testament. And the reason that the Bible is focused on Christ Jesus is because He is God in the flesh and He came to earth to save us. In the New Testament we learn about the personal and loving side of God as opposed to the "angry" God of the Old Testament. And although we are privileged to be able to receive the forgiveness of our sins and be brought back into the presence of God through the sacrifice of Jesus on the cross, this in no way changes God's laws. It fulfills them!

> Think not that I am come to destroy the law,
> or the prophets: I am not come to destroy, but
> to fulfil. 18 For verily I say unto you, 'Till
> heaven and earth pass, one jot or one tittle
> shall in no wise pass from the law, till all be
> fulfilled'.—Matthew 5:17-18

We are warned often in the New Testament to beware of false preachers and teachers who come with a message that says God has changed, that we don't need to repent, that He loves everyone just as they are and accepts sinful lifestyles and actions that make them happy.

Deception! Lies! This is NOT what God said in the Bible. God does not accept sin!

> Know ye not that the unrighteous shall not
> inherit the kingdom of God? Be not deceived:
> neither fornicators, nor idolaters, nor
> adulterers, nor effeminate (homosexuals), nor
> abusers of themselves with mankind, 10 Nor
> thieves, nor covetous, nor drunkards, nor
> revilers, nor extortioners, shall inherit the
> kingdom of God. 11 And such were some of
> you: but ye are washed, but ye are sanctified,
> but ye are justified in the name of the Lord
> Jesus, and by the Spirit of our God.—1
> Corinthians 6:9-11

The Bible says that people who don't want to reverence God and follow His rules have "itching ears". They want to find a church where the preacher says it's okay to do the sinful things that they enjoy doing. After all, in their mind if the preacher says it's okay, then that's all that counts. Foolishly, they don't study the scriptures themselves to know the truth, and so they justify their sin by following a preacher instead of God. But God says that anyone who does not repent, turn from their sins and follow Christ is NOT going to inherit the kingdom of God. They are not a Christian. They are someone who has been deceived, whose heart and mind is not given to God and who, sadly, will still be judged according to their sin.

> I marvel that ye are so soon removed from him that called you into the grace of Christ unto another gospel: 7 Which is not another; but there be some that trouble you, and would pervert the gospel of Christ. 8 But though we, or an angel from heaven, preach any other gospel unto you than that which we have preached unto you, let him be accursed. 9 As we said before, so say I now again, if any man preach any other gospel unto you than that ye have received, let him be accursed. 10 For do I now persuade men, or God? or do I seek to please men? for if I yet pleased men, I should not be the servant of Christ.—Galatians 1:6-10

The ONLY gospel to follow is the gospel of Jesus Christ! We need to follow our heart into truth and not our lusts through itching ears.

> For the time will come when they will not endure sound doctrine; but after their own lusts shall they heap to themselves teachers, having itching ears; 4And they shall turn away their ears from the truth, and shall be turned unto fables.—2 Timothy 4:3-4

Don't be Deceived!

Many of today's Christians have a very worldly point-of-view regarding the many kinds of sin that have become the norm in today's society. It's a view that is deceiving thousands of people every day because false teachers are watering down the truth to blend with an evil society. But it doesn't matter what people think or what people deem should be acceptable; we need to know what God says is acceptable and what God says is sin. People are no longer being led by their heart, but rather by their lusts. And because of this, they choose to follow a modern-day god and don't even realize that they are being deceived.

> Know ye not that the unrighteous shall not inherit the kingdom of God? Be not deceived: neither fornicators, nor idolaters, nor adulterers, nor effeminate, nor abusers of themselves with mankind, 10 Nor thieves, nor covetous, nor drunkards, nor revilers, nor extortioners, shall inherit the kingdom of God.—1 Corinthians 6:9-10

Most of us will acknowledge that many of these acts are sin and we wouldn't even look in that direction to consider participating in them. We are aware that to have a sexual affair outside of our marriage is adultery or that to go to a bar and drool over some seductive person could lead us into fornication, and so we don't even consider it. However, God mentioned some sins in this scripture that many fall prey to without being fully aware of it, and so we need to become aware and not allow our fleshly desires to commit sins against God.

Stealing is something that none of us would do deliberately because we know it's wrong, and yet some of the things we do can still brand us as a thief. Some of us enjoy a full social life and so at work we'll spend time chatting with co-workers about personal issues. Or perhaps we'll spend excessive time talking on the phone or sending e-mails or texts to our friends. We had agreed with the employer that we would submit ourselves to our job for our wages, and yet we use up some of this work time for social purposes. Are we not "stealing" time and money?

> Thou therefore which teachest another, teachest thou not thyself? thou that preachest a man should not steal, dost thou steal?— Romans 2:21

It may seem petty, but we are preaching one thing and doing another, just like Apostle Paul said. And our excuse is that everyone does it and so we're just following the crowd. But in doing this we're guilty of both stealing and lying because this is not what the employer is paying us to do.

Idolatry is a word that most Christians hate because we all believe that God should be the only one we worship, and yet He has a lot of competition among His own children. Many of us don't even realize that we have a love for money or things that is equal to or greater than our love for God. Some of us are more devoted to our favorite sports than we are to Him, and others of us live for our weekly television series and base all of our thoughts and conversations around them. It's one thing to have interests in different things in this life, but it's quite another to make them more important and more preferred than spending time in worship and prayer with God, or in reading and studying the scriptures. It's more than just balancing out our priorities; it's making God our only priority. When we put God first, He is faithful to supply all of our needs so our main focus doesn't have to be on things; it can be on Him.—Philippians 4:19.

Excessive drinking has become an issue for many of us. Apostle Paul said in1 Timothy 5:23 that a little wine for a sick stomach or for an ill person is good because it numbs the body and helps relieve the pain. But many of us have abused that suggestion and alcohol has become a grocery staple in our home. We depend on it to get us through the challenges of life rather than depending on God. But more than that, some of us like to indulge in it so that we can enjoy the total freedom of thought that it gives. Yet, God has told us in Ephesians 5:18 not to drink to excess and not to get drunk.

Coveting material possessions has become almost impossible to not do with the advertising world flaunting exciting things in our face all the time. The commercials on TV and in magazines make things look so desirable that we just have to have them, and so we become unappreciative of what we do have as we strive to get more—bigger, better, fancier and more technical—even though what we already have works perfectly. God tells us in Matthew 6:19-20 that we should not make earthly possessions our treasures. This "greed" attitude is what has almost bankrupted our country. Few of us can keep up with the cost and so we use "charge cards" and we run up debts that we can't pay. We work longer hours to meet our financial obligations and then we become stressed and live on medications—and all because we covet something instead of waiting on God to see if this is what HE wants for us.

Revilers are people who like to stir up trouble. Matthew 5:9 says we are to be peacemakers, but the tensions of this world and the pressures and challenges that beset us each day are slowly breaking down our ability to be peaceful. There are times when some of us lose it and speak unkind words in very loud disagreements. Others feel justified in their aggressive view points because they know their political and social rights and take active roles to defend them. And still others get caught up with gossiping, but call it's called "discussing" something or someone, and so they feel justified in their actions. We need to remember that we represent God in all things and that He said we are to be peacemakers, which means we don't cause trouble or aggravate people, but rather, we strive for peace. Our opinion is just that, and our job is to promote God's ways by encouraging peace so that the enemy doesn't get any glory in the tribulation we're enduring.

Homosexuality is legal in this world, but it's an abomination to God. We cannot just accept it as the norm when we know that God is sickened by it. Yet, it has slowly and surely crept in to become a norm in our society and is even being deemed as acceptable in some of our churches. We're being taught to love everyone and to judge no one and so we accept the sin in people as not being our problem. But we have to stay focused on God and study the scriptures so we'll know the truth. God tells us to hate sin and to have no part of it. So, we have to realize that God's word stands way above what this world says. He made people to be male and female—Genesis 1:27 and He tells us in Leviticus 18:22 that man lying with man is an abomination and that those who do it should be punished. As Christians, we support what God says and not what this world condones.

We must always keep our eyes on God and study the scriptures so that we can know what is good and acceptable to God—2 Timothy 2:15. Judgment is coming to the people of this earth who don't know Jesus and who live in and enjoy a life of sin. We will all face eternity whether we want to believe it now or not. What we think doesn't matter; it's what God has said that will come to pass.

> And He said, 'Take heed that ye be not deceived: for many shall come in My name, saying, I am Christ; and the time draweth

near: go ye not therefore after them'.—Luke
21:8

Don't be deceived! People who deliberately indulge
in sin will never inherit God's kingdom, but they will be
judged by the law for breaking the law when they stand
before Christ on Judgment Day. But for Christians, deception
is the beginning of a lie that the devil wants us to believe. He
wants to take us away from God and so he tricks us into
thinking that God has changed with the world and that He
doesn't deem some things to be sin any more. He convinces
us to remain passive with the world and so we overlook the
sins so we can fit in a bit better. However, we are called to be
the Light of the world and we can only do that if the light of
God shines brightly through us in all the things we do. We
need to stay in the scriptures so that we know the truth. And
we need to be wise so that we're not deceived!

> Study to shew thyself approved unto God, a
> workman that needeth not to be ashamed,
> rightly dividing the word of truth.—2
> Timothy 2:15

Ronnie Dauber

Endorsing Sin Brings Judgment

God gave Moses some laws known as the Ten Commandments—found in Exodus 20— and these were to be the benchmark that would govern the people to keep them from sin so they follow God. These laws have been passed down throughout the years and are not unique to any particular community; they are God's governing laws for all of mankind everywhere. Any government that dares to defy God and endorse sin will bring judgment upon that nation!

People will stray from God and follow false gods— aka the devil in disguise—and they will choose to serve him through their own lusts and greed, but that does not give them the authority to change God's laws. In fact, it's total rebellion. God didn't give us a choice; He told us to obey them. There are no exceptions.

This attitude of endorsing sin is spreading rapidly throughout the nations. The people petition the governments and the governments respond by catering to their desires and changing God's laws to meet today's "needs". It authorizes the changes and the people cheer them on and continue to bring more petitions for change. It's a rebellious cycle that is bringing damnation upon this world as it drifts closer and closer towards judgment.

We read in 2 Timothy 3:16 that, "All scripture is given by inspiration of God". The content of the scriptures is not what people thought or assumed, but is what God told them to write. Hebrews 13:8 says, "Jesus Christ the same yesterday, and today, and forever." Nowhere in the Bible does it even suggest that God could or would ever change what He told the patriarchs to write. In fact, in Revelations 22:18-19 God warns of the danger that will come to anyone who changes even one word of scripture. Whatever God said

70

in the scriptures is what God meant when He instructed them to be written, and it's what God means now.

Throughout the Old Testament we see that God poured His wrath onto the people and literally destroyed them because of their sin—(the flood, Sodom & Gomorrah, the rebels of Moses). They worshipped other idols, lived and promoted immorality including sexual perversion (homosexuality), and murdered and sacrificed their children to their gods. Oh how sinful! So deserving of God's wrath! And yet—is the world today any different from then?

It seems to be far less barbaric today and much more civilized—or so we dare to think. But while most of the laws of God are being modified in one way or another, there are two particular laws that have been rewritten by the world's legal system to appease the ungodly people in it. These changes not only give us licence to disobey God, but they completely change the value and integrity of life. Jesus gave His life to save the people, and today people are sacrificing lives of others to save themselves.

1) Thou shalt not kill—Exodus 20:13

When God said we should not murder, He meant just that. He wasn't talking about casualties of war; He was talking about life in general and He said that we are not to take the life of any other person. Yet, it's being done every day and it's legal! And not only is it legal, but we pay for it through our health care system.

Every day thousands of innocent babies are murdered. The world calls it abortion, but God calls it murder! People feel justified by their actions because "it is legal" and therefore, there's nothing wrong with it. No guilt. No shame. Totally legal! God's law has been modified for today's lifestyle and so life is good to those who are deceived and

71

ignorant of the truth. They don't see the victim as being a child with a beating heart who feels the torture of the abortion process. And just to clear the conscience of anyone who might be hesitant, the terminology has been changed to sound less demeaning. So, the law calls this a "process" known as "aborting a fetus", but God calls it "murdering a child." Yes, God calls the unborn child "life" not a fetus. We were once sickened by the ancient customs of sacrificing children to gods, yet people today still sacrifice children to the god of this world through their own lusts. There is no difference!

> Yea, they sacrificed their sons and their daughters unto devils, 38 And shed innocent blood, even the blood of their sons and of their daughters, whom they sacrificed unto the idols of Canaan: and the land was polluted with blood.—Psalm 106:37-38

2) Thou shalt not lie with mankind, as with womankind— Leviticus 18:22

There are many scriptures that clearly state that God forbids homosexuality. He says plainly that He made them male and female—Genesis 1:27. And verse 28 tells us that He told them to be fruitful and multiply and to have dominion over every living thing on the earth. And verse 31 says that at the end of the sixth day—at the end of all of His creating—God rested. Nothing new was made after the sixth day.

Therefore, people who choose to be transgender are defying God's creation. They aren't a "new" creation. But the world wants to engage in this immoral activity and so what better way to do it than to have the earthly law changed to allow it? So now being a transgender person is as legal and acceptable as all natural males and females, and the acceptance is being taught to our children in the public school system! And unfortunately, we Christians who do speak out against it are being called "haters" because we defend the laws and integrity of God. But we don't hate the people; it's these sinful behaviors that we will not support.

God forbids immorality! He was specific when He said that men were not to have sex with men, but to appease the sinful hearts of the people the earthly laws are changing God's law to say that it's okay now. The reason for the change is that the people insist that we're in a different time zone and that God's laws are outdated—if in fact, God is even real in the first place. So now, homosexual behavior is legal in many countries today, and as well, same-sex marriages are legal. The governments of this world took upon themselves the authority to redefine marriage. However, no one has the authority to redefine any part of God's laws, and that includes marriage.

> If a man also lie with mankind, as he lieth with a woman, both of them have committed an abomination: they shall surely be put to death; their blood shall be upon them.— Leviticus 20:13

> Do you not know that the unrighteous will not inherit the kingdom of God? Do not be deceived. Neither fornicators, nor idolaters, nor adulterers, nor homosexuals, nor sodomites, 10 nor thieves, nor covetous, nor drunkards, nor revilers, nor extortioners will inherit the kingdom of God.—1 Corinthians 6:9-10 NKJV

As Christians, we cannot support anything that contradicts the scriptures. When we endorse such behavior by even just accepting it and not standing against it, we risk putting ourselves in danger. Jesus told us that we are to preach the gospel and get people saved, not agree with their sin so we don't get people upset. People won't like what we have to say, but if we represent God, we have to say it anyway!

> And ye shall be hated of all men for my name's sake: but he that endureth to the end shall be saved.—Matthew 10:22

When we deliberately go against the laws of God to appease our modern-day lifestyle, we bring upon ourselves destruction and judgment. God wants us to follow Him and to be obedient to His word. He hates immorality and has told us that those who sinfully engage in it will not see the Kingdom of God—will not receive salvation unless they repent and come to Him with a clean heart.

God judged many nations in the Old Testament and destroyed them because of their sins. Do we really think that because we live in a more civilized time that God's judgment won't come to us? It's coming and the only way we will escape it is to repent of all our sins and follow Jesus—not the universal Jesus that accepts everyone and every sin without repentance, but the Jesus of the Bible who died on the cross and pardoned our sins, and who will forgive us for our sins when we repent and follow Him.

> If my people, which are called by my name, shall humble themselves, and pray, and seek my face, and turn from their wicked ways; then will I hear from heaven, and will forgive their sin, and will heal their land.—2 Chronicles 7:14

Fooling Ourselves

It seems at times that our lives are never-ending battle grounds where we fight one trial after another. Sometimes we sit back and wonder just what is going on! As Christians, shouldn't our lives just flow with ease and prosperity as some preachers proclaim it should? Are we missing something in our Christian walk or are we just fooling ourselves?

The truth is that we will have trials and tribulations in this world, and Jesus makes this clear in John 16:33 when He says, "In the world ye shall have tribulation" so it's wrong to think that we won't. The Lord does not delight in this; He doesn't get a thrill because we are having problems, but He often allows these things to come at us so we can learn and grow through them. It's when we face these challenges that we realize how weak we are on our own merits, and how much we need to pour our confidence and trust into God to deliver us through them.

Sometimes things come at us and we want to be responsible, and we actually think that we can handle them on our own. We feel that it's not something we need to bother God with and so we struggle through them alone. It might be a seemingly trivial family issue or a small financial setback, or even a case of the flu. These are challenges and we don't like them, but we don't want to ask God for help because we feel we can handle it on our own, or that it's too silly to ask God for. In other words, we suffer through them because our pride gets in the way.

> Pride goeth before destruction, and an haughty spirit before a fall.—(Proverbs 16:18).

God tells us to ask Him for anything and He will help us with it. We need to take all of our problems to God because there is no problem too great or too small, too profound or too trivial for God. He tells us to come to Him with these issues because He loves us and He wants us to be free of the things that weigh us down. He doesn't want us to try and battle against the devil on our own because He knows that on our own we cannot win.

> Casting all your care upon Him; for He careth for you.—1 Peter 5:7

> And whatsoever ye shall ask in my name, that will I do, that the Father may be glorified in the Son. 14 If ye shall ask any thing in my name, I will do it.—John 14:13-14

When we realize that our life is not our own, our walk with God matures and we become more dependent upon God. When we have needs or when problems come at us, we need to give them to God right away and wait on Him for the answer. When we do, God is able to work on our behalf and the answer will come. But more than getting the answer to our problem is the fact that through each tribulation our faith in God grows, and our dependency upon Him becomes greater so that there is more of Him and less of us in our heart. We begin to realize our own weaknesses as we allow His strength in us to grow.

Apostle Paul teaches us that it's Christ in us who gives us our strength. We can't learn it or develop it on our own; it's not about theology. It's our faith and trust in God [who lives in us] that makes us strong. When we came to the cross, we accepted the salvation of Jesus because we acknowledged that we could not save ourselves—that He was our Redeemer—and now we realize as we grow that He is our strength.

> Therefore I take pleasure in infirmities, in reproaches, in necessities, in persecutions, in

distresses for Christ's sake: for when I am
weak, then am I strong.—2 Corinthians 12:10

We need to stop thinking that we can do it ourselves
and start depending upon God. His Holy Spirit in us gives us
the wisdom and the strength we need when we study the
Bible and get fed by God's word. He will get us through the
trials because He has already defeated the enemy at the cross
and so our battle has already been won. But if we fight the
devil on our own, it's a new battle and we will likely lose.
And if by chance we do succeed, we are more likely to take
the credit ourselves than give all the glory to God.

I can do all things through Christ who
strengthens me.—Philippians 4:13 NKJV

As we study the Bible and learn about God, problems
will come at us, and they are often the means that God uses
to teach us lessons and to draw us closer to Him. And often,
He allows them for our own benefit so that we can show
ourselves where our trust and confidence lies—in Him or in
ourselves. If we can actually give the problems to God when
they come and thank Him and trust Him for His direction, we
mature as our confidence in God grows a little bit more with
each trial.

When we try to tackle the situations on our own
accord, we actually raise ourselves up and deny God's
strength in us and that stunts our growth. When we became
Christians, that old man in us died and our lives were given
to the Lord. It's no longer our life to live how we want; we
have given our lives to serve Him and He lives in us, so we
need to let Him live in us.

I have been crucified with Christ; it is no
longer I who live, but Christ lives in me; and
the life which I now live in the flesh I live by

> faith in the Son of God, who loved me and gave Himself for me.—Galatians 2:20 NKJV

> Or do you not know that your body is the temple of the Holy Spirit who is in you, whom you have from God, and you are not your own? For you were bought at a price; therefore glorify God in your body and in your spirit, which are God's.—1 Corinthians 6:19-20 NKJV

We are no match on our own human level for the powers of darkness. We need God in us to get us through each and every trial in life—and don't be fooled; the devil will bring us lots of challenges and never allow us win over them, small or not! We need God's wisdom and strength to confront him. Our faith in Christ in us gets stronger with each trial we give to God. And we become mature Christians who know that we can trust God for every aspect of our lives, and each problem we overcome through Christ becomes a stepping stone for the next problem that may be even bigger.

This world gets more corrupt every day as it pushes closer towards judgment. We need the strength and power within us to come from Christ alone. God wants us to be mature Christians who know that it is Him in us who gives us the strength, the wisdom and the ability to overcome trials. People need to see Christ in us if we are going to lead them into salvation. All glory must be to God and not to our own abilities because it's not in own strength that we do anything.

> Trust in the Lord with all your heart, And lean not on your own understanding; 6 In all your ways acknowledge Him, And He shall direct your paths.—Proverbs 3:5-6 NKJV

When we try to get through the trials on our own merits, we won't develop our faith in Christ because we will not have put our faith to work—(James 2:20), and we won't know that we can trust Him. We may think that we are maturing as Christians because we think we believe, but the truth is that if we don't put our faith to work and depend on Christ to get us through our trials, that it's still us in control. If we proclaim that we are Christians but don't allow God to fight our battles because we think we can do it on our own, we are only fool ourselves.

> These things I have spoken unto you, that in me ye might have peace. In the world ye shall have tribulation: but be of good cheer; I have overcome the world.—John 16:33

God Does NOT Tolerate Compromise!

The true doctrine of "Christianity" has been watered-down and changed radically in today's world. In fact, the word "Christianity" has become a generic term used to describe the many beliefs that all involve the name "Jesus", but don't necessarily teach the Gospel of Christ. The so-called Christian leaders are violating the laws of God by teaching false doctrines and making a total mockery out of the Bible! The truth is: God does NOT tolerate compromise!

Many people want all the perks that come with being a being a Christian, but they don't want to part from the sins of this world or submit to God and receive Christ as their Lord and Savior. They like to be in control. Why? Because unknowing to them, this world is governed by a devil that rebelled against God and also refused to submit to His authority. He rules this world in a crusade against God and this same rebellious thinking is in all those who follow him.

> We wrestle not against flesh and blood, but against principalities, against powers, against the rulers of the darkness of this world, against spiritual wickedness in high places.— Ephesians 6:12

Inside each of us is a hidden desire to find the one who created us. And so God has set out believers to cross the paths of each one of us so that we can hear the truth and have that yearning answered. But sadly, many will hear, but before they are committed to the Lord, the devil will show up and deceive them into following a false path.

> For many are called, but few are chosen.— Matthew 22:14

So it's no wonder that people will either reject Christ entirely or accept a false doctrine when that seed of faith is given to them. Because their desires are so strong, many will be easily convinced that God will give them everything because they are a "king's kid" and they deserve it. And with this wrong desire to seek God, many will get what they deserve, but not what they expect!

They will pay the price for their sin throughout eternity because they dared to lift themselves up above God instead of submitting themselves to Him, just as the devil did. In Acts 8:18-20 a man named Simon came to Peter to offer him money to receive the Holy Spirit. Peter's response was, "Thy money perish with thee, because thou hast thought that the gift of God may be purchased with money."

There is NO compromise when it comes to the gospel. Satan challenged God and lost. And those who are also foolish enough to challenge Him will also lose!

God loves us and He wants us to be with Him throughout eternity. He created the law as a guideline so we could know what sin is and then not do it. Then He permitted animal sacrifices as atonements for our sin because as much as the best person tried, it was impossible not to sin. Eventually, Jesus came as the ultimate sacrifice, the Lamb of God, to take away the sins of the world—John 1:29.

Romans 3:23 says that we have all sinned and we're all guilty and worthy of punishment. If there is sin in us when we face God on Judgment Day, we'll be judged by the Law of God (Ten Commandments), and we will suffer the consequences of our sins. But God doesn't want that for anyone and so He has provided our salvation whereby we can have the sin forgiven and live with Him throughout eternity.

> For the wages of sin is death; but the gift of
> God is eternal life through Jesus Christ our
> Lord.—Romans 6:23

God came to earth in the form of a man and He gave His physical body as a sacrifice on that cross so He could take upon Himself all of our sins and pay the punishment for those sins. This means that we are free and that when we die we won't stand before Christ to be judged by the law because we are no longer under the law. We are now under grace and covered by the righteousness of Christ.

> For sin shall not have dominion over you: for
> ye are not under the law, but under grace.—
> Romans 6:14

Are we all automatically saved? No. God provided our salvation by shedding His blood for us on the cross, but now it is up to each of us to accept Jesus as our Savior. We need to repent for our sins and turn from the sinful world to serve Him as Lord. Then we are saved! Then we are filled with His Spirit, and then we are Christians! We are freed from the punishment that will come to those who still belong to the world, who still serve the devil instead of God. But we Christians are no longer of this world for we now have the kingdom of God in us.

> Then Peter said unto them, 'Repent, and be
> baptized every one of you in the name of
> Jesus Christ for the remission of sins, and ye
> shall receive the gift of the Holy Ghost'.—
> Acts 2:38

The second we become saved, we are "born again"! Our old spirit dies and God fills us with His Spirit so we are changed inside. And as we study the Bible, worship and pray, we become more like our Father and the scriptures become alive in us. The gospel of Christ becomes our only doctrine!

> Therefore if any man be in Christ, he is a new
> creature: old things are passed away; behold,

all things are become new.—2 Corinthians 5:17

So if people can change the meaning of the scriptures, ignore some of them or add new revelations, we have to realize that they are not being led by God because the Holy Spirit teaches only truth: He does NOT compromise it. But the devil does! And through deception he's turning people away from the true God of Heaven. Many see God as a servant who's there to bless them; others see Him as a modern-day congenial God who now accepts people just as they are without repentance because they believe that Jesus saved "everyone" on the cross; and still others see Him as a cruel God who demands us to fear Him or else.

God loves us each of us enough to send Jesus to save us, but it's only those who accept His salvation and are born again that are saved from the judgment to come. Time is running out and we need to get serious about who we will serve. God is real and eternity is forever. We can accept Jesus now or bow in shame to Him later. We can live throughout eternity with Him or be tormented in hell with the devil. There is only one gospel; only one way to Heaven. Flee deception and follow Jesus while there's still time!

Because when it comes to the gospel, God does NOT tolerate compromise!

And if it seem evil unto you to serve the Lord, choose you this day whom ye will serve; whether the gods which your fathers served that were on the other side of the flood, or the gods of the Amorites, in whose land ye dwell: but as for me and my house, we will serve the Lord.—Joshua 24:15

Stop! God is not Deaf

As Christians, we take our concerns to God in prayer and this is what we should do, but unfortunately, many prayers become a repeated routine where we ask the same thing, day after day. By the millionth prayer we wonder if God even hears us as our petitions get stronger and our faith gets weaker. What many don't understand is that He heard us the first time—so stop because God is not deaf!

Proverbs 15:29 tells us that, "The Lord hears the prayer of the righteous." Yet many will ask, "Well, if He hears us, why doesn't He answer us? Is He too busy? Are our problems too small?" No, nothing is too hard for God or impossible for Him. He is Omnipresent, which means He is everywhere at the same time and He is not confined to our time or place. He's Omniscient, which means He knows everything about everything and is very able to answer every single prayer from everyone at the same time—and in a personal way. God is Omnipotent, which means He is all-powerful, supreme and unstoppable, so there is nothing and no one who can stop Him for doing anything—except us.

There are five basic questions that your must consider when it seems that God doesn't answer prayers:

1) Are you a Christian?

Many people have a vague knowledge of God and Heaven and refer to themselves as Christians. They accept that He's up there somewhere and when they need help they pray and assume that God will stop what He's doing and cater to them. But they don't know Him and don't honor Him and to their surprise, He doesn't answer, and that's because God does not acknowledge the prayers of the unsaved.

> The Lord is far from the wicked, But He hears
> the prayer of the righteous.—Proverbs 15:29
> NKJV

Who are the righteous? They are the people who realize they are sinners in need of a Savior. They are the ones who accept Jesus as their Lord and Savior, repent of their sins and get washed and made righteous in the shed blood of the Lamb. And they are the ones who are filled with God's Spirit, study the Bible and spend time in worship and prayer with the Lord. They are ones who are called "Christians".

> The next day John saw Jesus coming toward
> him, and said, 'Behold! The Lamb of God
> who takes away the sin of the world!'—John
> 1:29 NKJV

They are the ones who talk to God as a child would talk to their father, and they are the ones who God hears when they pray.

2) Do you have faith or doubt?

Many Christians have accepted Christ as their Savior and have been forgiven for their sins, but they don't know Him very well. They are too busy with the things of this world and spend little time reading the Bible or praising God. They don't know what He can and will do, and have not developed their faith to trust Him to answer their prayers.

The only way to know God is to study the scriptures and to learn of the history of God's people and how they rebelled against Him, and how through His love and patience toward them, He kept His outstretched arm over them until the Messiah would come in the New Testament. We learn about the love of God through Jesus, and so our faith, reverence and trust grow in Him, and all doubt disappears so that we can truly walk in faith and not by sight.

> Be diligent to present yourself approved to
> God, a worker who does not need to be
> ashamed, rightly dividing the word of truth.—
> 2 Timothy 2:15 NKJV

But Christians who don't take the time to know the
God of their salvation can only walk by sight because they
don't know God enough to trust Him with their problems.
God hears them when they pray, but they don't know Him
enough to believe Him for the answer, so they don't really
look for the answer. And some might accept that God hears
them and will even wait for the answer, but they'll miss it
because it might not come the way they told God to bring it.

> For we walk by faith, not by sight—2
> Corinthians 5:7

3) Could the Answer be "No"?

Sometimes Christians ask God for things and just
assume that they know everything about their situation so
that all God needs to do is trust their judgment and give them
what they're asking for. They claim scriptures such as John
14:14 where it says to ask for anything in His name, and then
feel justified in asking for something like winning the lottery.
But God doesn't always want for us what we want for us. He
sees the big picture; He knows our future and His plan for us,
and He sees whether or not what we're asking for would be a
blessing or a curse to us.

> For as the heavens are higher than the earth,
> so are my ways higher than your ways, and
> my thoughts than your thoughts.—Isaiah 55:9

Too often we're grieved by situations around us; we
lose a loved one to cancer or to a tragedy; we become ill
ourselves; or we face financial stress that seems beyond our
ability to handle. We seek God for the answer, but the one He

86

gives is not the one we were expecting—and that's because we see only the scene in front of us and He sees the whole picture. Sometimes the answer is "No." But we need to trust Him and praise Him anyway because regardless of what we see or feel, He has everything in control.

> And we know that all things work together for good to them that love God, to them who are the called according to his purpose.—Romans 8:28

4) Are You Praying According to God's Will?

Many Christians live only in their own space and don't want to see the big picture. God has His plan for this world already set out and it's going just the way He said it would. The book of Revelation tells us what we can expect and what the outcome of this world will be. Satan brought sin into God's world through Adam, and God has provided the defeat of sin and death through Jesus to all who will accept it.

As we study the scriptures we learn what God likes, what He accepts and what He won't allow. We understand His law and the need for salvation, and we learn how patient, forgiving and merciful God is. Our knowledge and wisdom increases in the things of God, and our priorities become like His. Our heart becomes changed daily and we begin to see through His eyes. So when we pray, we ask for things that we know is in line with His will according to the scriptures, and then we no longer hope for an answer, but we look for the answer because we know that He means what He says.

> So shall my word be that goeth forth out of my mouth: it shall not return unto me void, but it shall accomplish that which I please, and it shall prosper in the thing whereto I sent it.—Isaiah 55:11

We no longer pray for prosperity for ourselves, but for our needs to be met, and for the salvation and for the needs of others.

5) Are You Praising God and Thanking Him?

We need to always remain humble and with a grateful heart toward God. The promise of salvation was given to the Jews first and then to the Gentiles, and through His love for us He gave His earthly body as sacrifice for our sins, and now we have been grafted into His family. God is faithful to His word, and when we ask for something we must realize that He heard us the first time and so we need to come to Him daily praising Him and thanking Him for the answer. It may come right away or it may take a while, but we praise God because He will bring it to pass on His timing. We just need to trust Him.

> Be careful for nothing; but in everything by prayer and supplication with thanksgiving let your requests be made known unto God.— Philippians 4:6

God is not deaf! He loves us and wants us to fellowship with Him. He wants us to cast all of our cares upon Him because He cares so much for us, and then He wants us to trust Him for the answer and praise Him for it.

How to be God's Influence in this World

Apostle Paul tells us that we need to confess our faith to be saved—Romans 10:9. But we're also told in James 2:20 that we need to put our faith to works because faith without works is dead. The only way that we can be a positive influence for Christ in this world is through our faith.

There are nine things we need to do to be a positive influence:

We need to give thanks: We give God thanks and praise because as we submit ourselves to God, we become more bonded with Him. It builds us up spiritually so that our heart is always looking to God for His love and faithfulness. When we don't give Him thanks and praise, a small void begins to grow and the devil is able to slip in and discourage us. We are more susceptible to his influence and to doubt. And so we not only give God thanks privately with our worship and praises, but also publically so others can see that we give Him thanks and praise from a joyful heart that is not broken in spite of the trials that attack us.

> In everything give thanks: for this is the will
> of God in Christ Jesus.—1 Thessalonians 5:18

We need to love each other: God tells us that we are to love each other—not put each other down and dissect each other as if we were science projects—but we are to love our brothers and sisters in Christ in spite of their faults or short comings. Not only does this give God great joy when He sees us working together in love, but it also has a mighty impact on the people around us. When the people of the world see or hear Christians backbiting they don't see Christ in us, but rather, just another conflicting group of religious bigots and they'll avoid us and definitely not want to become one of us, thus possibly missing out on salvation.

> A new commandment I give unto you, That
> ye love one another; as I have loved you, that
> ye also love one another. 35 By this shall all
> men know that ye are my disciples, if ye have
> love one to another.—John 13:34-35 (NKJV)

We need to forgive each other: Sometimes we get a little self-righteous and feel we have the right to treat others badly because of offences they have committed against us. Instead of treating them as God treats us with His love and forgiveness, we allow these offences to actually become a stumbling block that separates us from God. This self-righteous attitude belongs to the world and they'll quickly sense it and mock our testimony for Christ because of it. If God can forgive us for our sins that nailed Him to the cross, then surely we can forgive others who have hurt us and treat them with the same loving kindness that God bestows upon us—because we may be Christians, but we are still sinners, saved by grace.

> But if ye forgive not men their trespasses,
> neither will your Father forgive your
> trespasses.—Matthew 6:15 (NKJV)

We don't judge each other: God told us in 1 John 4:1 that we are to judge doctrines and teachers of doctrines by comparing their teaching to the scriptures. This way we'll know if they are preaching truth or a false doctrine, and if it's false, we need to be ready to warn others. However, God has not given us the right to judge anyone's life, much less determine if they'll go to Heaven or to hell. Only He knows the heart of man and only He will open the Book of Life to read whose names are in there—and that book hasn't been opened yet! We need to be careful that we don't focus on the faults of others more than on our own faults, and more than on the forgiveness of God. When we judge others, we separate ourselves from God and we become a stumbling block for those watching.

> Judge not, that you be not judged. 2 For with what judgment you judge, you will be judged; and with the measure you use, it will be measured back to you. 3 And why do you look at the speck in your brother's eye, but do not consider the plank in your own eye?— Matthew 7:1-3

We need to be patient with other: We sometimes forget what other people are going through or that they may not know or understand God as we do, and some of us are quick to lose our patience with them. But this is not God's will. After all, when we look at our own lives truthfully, we'll see that throughout our Christian life we have messed up many times, and yet God has always remained patient with us. He doesn't expect us to be perfect because that won't happen until we're with Jesus, but we He does expect us to treat others the way we want to be treated; the way God treats us. And that means being patient and kind to others regardless of how we feel.

> Now we exhort you, brethren, warn those who are unruly, comfort the fainthearted, uphold the weak, be patient with all.—1 Thessalonians 5:14 (NKJV)

We need to realize that we are all sinners: Each Christian lives every day in God's grace and we need to realize that it's only because of His love and grace that we are saved. Not one of us deserves a home in Heaven with Jesus, but He loves us so much that He was willing to die in our place—John 3:16—so we would be free of all sin and be with Him throughout eternity. That should humble each of us to an attitude of gratitude so that we don't exalt ourselves above anyone else, remembering that we, too, are still a sinner who's been forgiven and saved by grace.

> For for all have sinned and fall short of the glory of God.—Romans 3:23

We need to sow mercy: When God's spirit lives in us our personality and characteristics become like His, and it's natural for us to have a kind, gentle heart that treats others as Christ treats us. He has shown us mercy through the cross and we need to show mercy to others, as well. If God didn't have mercy toward us, we would not be saved in the first place. And it's because of His love and mercy for us that He watches over us every second of our lives and HE strives to bring us to the scriptures so we can truly know what a wonderful, loving Father we have. We really do reap what we sow, and we need to sow mercy.

> Be ye therefore merciful, as your Father also is merciful.—Luke 6:36

We need to give without expecting anything in return: Our salvation is a gift from God. He gave it to us because He loves us and there is nothing we can give Him in return that could possibly equal what He's given to us. Yet, we can show our love and our gratitude and bring Him great joy through our actions of love and grace towards others. We can pray for people, help them physically or financially, encourage them, be a friend to them and even offer them gifts with a heart that does not expect anything back. People of this world give and then look for a return, but we are Christians. We don't expect the people of this world to pay it back. We do all we do to the glory of God because we love Him and we want to share this love with others.

> Freely you have received, freely give.— Matthew 10:8 (NKJV)

We need to pray for those who come against us: Sometimes it's really easy to hate those who come against us and hurt us. Yet, God wants us to pray for them, not avenge them. Our prayers not only bring peace to us in a stressful situation, but they may cause those who give us the stress to come to Christ. God tells us to love our enemies—not that we should bring them into our homes and become like them, but that we should realize that if they knew God, they would not attack us. So through our prayers God can change their hearts and they can even get saved. We don't speak badly about them when they bother us and we don't stir up trouble. Our peaceful attitude can be a great influence to the world because of His love in us.

> But I say to you, love your enemies, bless those who curse you, do good to those who hate you, and pray for those who spitefully use you and persecute you.— Matthew 5:44 (NKJV)

When we see people through God's eyes, we are able to be witnesses for Him everywhere we go, and a positive influence to the glory of God!

> That ye may be blameless and harmless, the sons of God, without rebuke, in the midst of a crooked and perverse nation, among whom ye shine as lights in the world.—Philippians 2:15

Be Doers and Not Hearers Only

This world is moving speedily toward its end and there is a lot going on around us that confirms things are changing—just as Jesus said they would in the last days. We are surrounded in escalating crime, horrendous acts of anti-Semitism, growing starvation and poverty, and uncontrollable immorality that is sponsored and promoted in every facet of the media around us. If ever there was a time when the gospel of Jesus and His hope of salvation needed to be heard, it's now! We need to become doers of the word and not hearers only.

> And Jesus answered and said unto them, 'Take heed that no man deceive you. 5 For many shall come in my name, saying, I am Christ; and shall deceive many. 6 And ye shall hear of wars and rumours of wars: see that ye be not troubled: for all these things must come to pass, but the end is not yet. 7 For nation shall rise against nation, and kingdom against kingdom: and there shall be famines, and pestilences, and earthquakes, in divers places. 8 All these are the beginning of sorrows'.—Matthew 24:4-8

It's getting obvious that God is no longer at the heart of man and that the world is living just as Jesus said it would in Matthew 24:38-39 (NKJV): "For as in the days before the flood, they were eating and drinking, marrying and giving in marriage, until the day that Noah entered the ark, and did not know until the flood came and took them all away, so also will the coming of the Son of Man be." The world has deliberately removed God from the schools, out of public gatherings, far from the work place and sadly, even from the church. It's not that God is not present or that He doesn't see because God is very present and He does see everything! It's that the people of the world don't want Him in their lives. And to add to this sorrow are the many Christians who know what's right, but don't take a stand for God.

Hundreds of thousands of people struggle every day for survival as storms and unusual weather catastrophes attack nations around the globe with a vengeance. People have drifted far away from God, yet they are quick to say that if there was a God, then he's a god of hate because He's not doing anything to help them. They have become too quick to blame God because He won't help when they expect that He should; but in all fairness, He has been told to stay out of their lives. Should He just hang in the balances and dive in when we bid Him and then get lost when it's inconvenient to have Him near us? Is He God or a puppet?

> And there is no creature hidden from His sight, but all things are naked and open to the eyes of Him to whom we must give account.—Hebrews 4:13 NKJV

It's really sad that so many people don't know Jesus and that their lives are ending in torment because they don't know that He can and will help them. But how will they know who God is if we don't tell them? The burden is on Christians! Jesus said in Matthew 5:14 that we are the light of the world. This means that we should shine in the darkness so those in that darkness can see the hope of God in us. What hope are we if we hide our light or if we just refuse to shine? The onus to preach the gospel and to show Jesus to the people of the world is on the Christians! It's not on televangelists or in modern-day doctrines, or in churches that prefer to glorify people instead of God. It's on each and every individual Christian.

When we got saved we repented of our sins and turned from the world's ungodly nature to follow Jesus. Then we were filled with His Spirit—the same Spirit that raised Christ from the dead! Jesus is the light in this dark world; one that is controlled by a dark being, namely the devil. And now, even though Jesus has risen into Heaven, through His Spirit in us we continue to shine that light in the darkness.

> But if the Spirit of Him that raised up Jesus from the dead dwell in you, He that raised up Christ from the dead shall also quicken your mortal bodies by His Spirit that dwelleth in you.—Romans 8:11

When God created the garden in Eden, He walked with Adam and Eve there until they rebelled, and then He left because God is Holy, and sin (and all people who are filled with sin) cannot be in the presence of His Holiness or it's destroyed. And God didn't want to stay apart from the children He'd created so He sent Jesus to redeem us back, and God's Spirit lived in Him and Jesus gave His Spirit to those who love Him so that once again, God was able to walk on the earth and communicate with His children. The very first people to receive His Spirit were Peter, along with the other ten disciples and all the followers on the Day of Pentecost.

> And when the day of Pentecost was fully come, they were all with one accord in one place. 2 And suddenly there came a sound from heaven as of a rushing mighty wind, and it filled all the house where they were sitting. 3 And there appeared unto them cloven tongues like as of fire, and it sat upon each of them. 4 And they were all filled with the Holy Ghost, and began to speak with other tongues, as the Spirit gave them utterance.—Acts 2:1-4

Peter tells us that when we become Christians God's Holy Spirit comes to live in us, too. Why? Because when we are washed in the blood of Jesus and forgiven for our sins, the old man (or spirit) in us dies and we are filled with new life; God's Spirit. We are born again—John 3:3. And it's only through His Holy Spirit that we can study the Bible and know the truth because He teaches us as we read. (On our own we read only words with our own interpretations of those words.) And when we are ready, we share that truth with others. It's only through His Spirit that we can worship God in truth, and that we can be the vessels of God in this world. With God's Spirit in us, we are united with God and He gives us the commission to preach the gospel and share the truth with others.

> Then Peter said unto them, 'Repent, and be baptized every one of you in the name of Jesus Christ for the remission of sins, and ye shall receive the gift of the Holy Ghost'.— Acts 2:38

Yet, while many Christians love the Lord and are filled with His Spirit, they don't want to get involved with teaching and preaching and working with others. They feel that this is the job of the pastor, but it's not. The pastor's job is to keep his congregation following and serving Christ. And not just so they can have a fruitful and prosperous life, but so that they can be the soldiers who go forth in the darkness of this world and fight for Christ! It's a congregation of people who preach and share the love of God with all of those around them. It's a congregation of people who will stand for righteousness and not back down, who will speak up and defend the integrity of God, and who will fight for His truth to prevail!

In many ways, Christians must share the blame for our country becoming so distant from God. When sin began to raise its ugly head, many Christians just shut up and said nothing. They didn't want to make a spectacle of themselves or stir the waters. They preferred to remain quiet in their little corner of the world, and just complain and talk about it behind closed doors. They should have stood boldly and fought against the acts of sin, but because they didn't, sin is quickly taking over everything we hold dear. Abortions might not have become the greatest act of murder ever devised, where hundreds of thousands of innocent lives are murdered LEGALLY every day. We wouldn't have the stench of immorality all around us because we would have taken a stand before it got to this point. We wouldn't have sex education in our public schools that's just short of pornography, or transgender people who have been accepted legally, forcing women's public bathrooms to allow men to enter. This corrupting sin is teaching our children that being gay is normal and that sexual activity among young teens is totally acceptable. Yet, to God is an abomination!

It's not too late, though. We still have time to pray diligently for our nation and for the protection of the Jewish nation. As long as we have today we still have time to take a stand for Christ! If we can't get out and preach, then we can support Godly ministries prayerfully and financially. We can speak up whenever possible, be a helping hand, be an encouragement, and be ready to share the gospel of Jesus wherever we go, without reservation and without shame. We need to be doers of the word now! Time is running out and Jesus is about to return. If the people of this world don't see God in us now, they won't see Him at all until they face Him on Judgment Day and then it will be too late!

> And He said unto them, 'Go ye into all the world, and preach the gospel to every creature'.—Mark 16:15

We are Strongest when we are Weak

There are many times when the trials and challenges of this life get us down and literally disable us from functioning with any clarity. We become tired and defeated because we get so weak. The world can't help us and family and friends don't seem to understand; we feel all alone with a problem that is overwhelming and there doesn't seem to be any way to get through it. Yet, there is hope because the Bible tells us that we are strongest when we are weak.

Many Christians forget to rest in the power of God, and instead, they quote scriptures diligently and plead their case before Him daily—and when nothing changes, they begin to lose their faith in God. And this is very sad because they are depending on their own merits to quote scripture and bring it to pass, but they don't have the revelation of those scriptures. Christians need to get the scriptures deep into their heart by studying them prayerfully every day. And then they can pray and bring God into remembrance of those scriptures and have faith in God to answer their prayers. If Christians are praying and don't really know God or the scriptures, they have no faith in Him and will get discouraged with the Lord.

The world we live in is very adamant about self-esteem and being all we can be. It doesn't teach us to be humble, but rather it encourages us to be independent people who can do anything that we put our minds to. This may be a good protocol for situations that we have complete control over, but it's useless information to hold on to when enduring situations that we have no control over.

We need to remember that this world is not one of chance; it's controlled by a very determined and powerfully evil devil who is a fallen angel from Heaven, and on our own merits we cannot defeat his powers. We will lose every single time we attempt it. He controls everything of sin in this world and people can't fight him. We know that angels have more power than people because it says in Hebrews 2:9 that Jesus was born a human who was a little lower than the angels. So when we think we can come against the powers of darkness on our own merits, we are being deceived.

While we can't fight against the devil on our own merits, God has provided a way that we can fight him. Jesus defeated the devil at the cross, and we are no longer under the curse of the law so we don't have to accept anything in our lives that is under the curse. When we can realize the power that was given to us by Jesus, through His Holy Spirit in us, we will realize that we can defeat the devil because our strength is not our own, it's in the power of the Word.

Sometimes we need to simply ignore what the devil is throwing at us and focus on God's word. We can even read the scriptures out loud and declare them to the heavens. This not only makes our faith in God stronger, but the devil sees our faith, and he knows that we truly believe the words we're reading and he flees. He does not want to be in the presence of the One who defeated him.

> Submit yourselves therefore to God. Resist the devil, and he will flee from you.—James 4:7

But, when trials come that require a fight, we need to be ready to fight! We cannot do this on our own and so when we get to this point, we become weak! So weak that we almost faint because we know that we can be defeated by this enemy. And yet, at the same time, we can become the strongest we've ever been through God's Spirit in us! When "we" step back and become the warriors that God has told us to be, we can and we will defeat the devil.

Now since the devil is a spirit, we need to fight him on his level and we do this only by putting on the whole armour of God. But first we need to study the scriptures prayerfully and diligently so we can know the truth will be planted deep into our heart. Our faith in God is made strong as we grow, and slowly we begin to put on the armour of God, and through it we will defeat the enemy.

> Finally, my brethren, be strong in the Lord, and in the power of his might.
>
> 11 Put on the whole armour of God, that ye may be able to stand against the wiles of the devil.
>
> 12 For we wrestle not against flesh and blood, but against principalities, against powers, against the rulers of the darkness of this world, against spiritual wickedness in high places.
>
> 13 Wherefore take unto you the whole armour of God, that ye may be able to withstand in the evil day, and having done all, to stand.
>
> 14 Stand therefore, having your loins girt about with truth, and having on the breastplate of righteousness;
>
> 15 And your feet shod with the preparation of the gospel of peace;
>
> 16 Above all, taking the shield of faith, wherewith ye shall be able to quench all the fiery darts of the wicked.
>
> 17 And take the helmet of salvation, and the sword of the Spirit, which is the word of God:

18 Praying always with all prayer and supplication in the Spirit, and watching thereunto with all perseverance and supplication for all saints;—Ephesians 6:10-18

When we know who we are in Christ and what He has done for us and what His plans are for us, then we become strong in Him. We will be filled with His wisdom and knowledge and we will know when to resist and when to fight, and how to fight according to God's will.

When we are attacked with a health issue, for example, we will know what God says about healing and that in Isaiah 53:5 it says, "By His stripes we are healed." And in Galatians 3:13 we learn that we are no longer under the curse because Christ became a curse for us. And in 2 Chronicles 7:14 we read that if we will turn to God and serve Him then He will heal us. This knowledge becomes the basis for our faith in God and we accept what God says and not what the world says. So, the wisdom and knowledge develop our faith in God and it becomes the armour that we use to fight the enemy. He will use the world system to defeat us by telling us that we will die from the cancer, or that this result will happen if we don't surrender to the world's toxic cures.

We will know the truth that we've studied in the scriptures and it will be deep inside us so we won't have any doubt; only trust in God that His words are true and that He is faithful to His words. And we will know who we are in Christ and that it's HIS righteousness that covers us and not our own self-righteousness that we think we have. And our feet will take us to places where we will continue to spread the gospel of peace to others who may be totally stressed out with our illness. The faith we have in God becomes our shield and when negative reports and discouragement tries to break us, we will speak the word of God boldly and the attacks will not hurt us because they're being bounced off through our faith in God's word. We'll have on our helmet of salvation and be reminded constantly that Jesus is our King and that we belong to Him and not to this world and so the ruler of this world has no authority over us. And the words we speak in faith will defeat the enemy because he knows that God is alive in us!

When we can realize that on our own merits we are weak, and that with His armour on us we are strong, then we can be the warriors that God has called us to be!

> But they that wait upon the Lord shall renew their strength; they shall mount up with wings as eagles; they shall run, and not be weary; and they shall walk, and not faint.—Isaiah 40:31

Losing our Drive to Obey God

The Christian world is changing! There are Christians today who don't study the Bible to know God because they just rely on the preacher to teach them everything they think they need to know! Then there are others who choose to follow one of the many so-called "Christian" doctrines because the "new" [false] gospel suits their needs, so they don't have to obey the "Old Testament God". As the modern-day church continues to blend cordially with a society that supports equality, free-will and even sin, it drifts further from God to please the people. What a dangerous path Christians travel when they lose their drive to obey God!

> Enter ye in at the strait gate: for wide is the gate, and broad is the way, that leadeth to destruction, and many there be which go in thereat.—Matthew 7:13

Somehow, modern-day "Christians" feel content to pick through the scriptures and accept the ones that please them and disregard the ones that don't. They feel justified as being Christians because they go to church, yet, they still live according to the world. They don't seek after God's Spirit to reveal the truth of the Bible to them and instead, feel that it's their right to choose what they'll believe. This, however, is what a religious person does; it is NOT what a Christian does. It is in the Christian's heart to obey God and this is because He has chosen to follow God.

> No man can serve two masters: for either he will hate the one, and love the other; or else he will hold to the one, and despise the other. Ye cannot serve God and mammon.—Matthew 6:24

Christians have come to the Lord because they realize that He is the King of the Earth, the promised Messiah who

104

sacrificed His earthly body as the ultimate offering to take away their sins so they could be free and forgiven and restored—saved from the judgment to come. They are filled with God's Holy Spirit when they repent and turn from the world to serve Him. The Christian heart has been changed from the desire to be part of the world into the joy that fills them because they belong to the Kingdom of God.

Christians take all their instruction from God through the scriptures, and gives all their praises and glory to Him alone. Christians do not allocate their lives to other people, or depend on an organized church or a rich and famous preacher for approval. Christians look only to God for every aspect of their lives. And, therefore, Christians follow only God by studying and believing the scriptures.

We know that the scriptures are written by men, but they weren't authored by men; God spoke through His Spirit to every man who produced their contribution of the scriptures, and each of them wrote what God told them to write. And so what better way to know God than to read the book that He wrote for us!

All scripture is given by inspiration of God, and is profitable for doctrine, for reproof, for correction, for instruction in righteousness.— 2 Timothy 3:16

God didn't give us a choice of what scriptures we should believe; He told us to study them all and get them deep into our heart. It's all or none! We can't get the fullness of the big picture that's written in the Bible unless we read and study and believe it all. And as we study, we become convicted of the things that aren't right in our lives before God and we are able to repent of those things and obediently follow Him; one issue at a time in most cases.

> Study to shew thyself approved unto God, a
> workman that needeth not to be ashamed,
> rightly dividing the word of truth.—2
> Timothy 2:15

However, those who aren't committed to God, but
who follow "religious people", haven't given their heart to
God and yet many of them still think that they are Christians.
They are taught man's interpretations of the scriptures and are
satisfied with that. They have no reverence, fear or respect
for God who wrote the scriptures and who will judge them
according to the laws in those scriptures, and that's because
they don't know Him. Yet, they'think they do.

> Beware of false prophets, which come to you
> in sheep's clothing, but inwardly they are
> ravening wolves.—Matthew 7:15

> For there shall arise false Christs, and false
> prophets, and shall shew great signs and
> wonders; insomuch that, if it were possible,
> they shall deceive the very elect.—Matthew
> 24:24

When we study the Bible, its truth becomes part of us
and we constantly shed hidden sins in our lives in obedience
to God as we grow. We make these changes because the
more we study, the more we become convicted of things that
are still wrong in our life, and before each change we realize
that we need to turn from them and obey God. But when we
struggle to obey or choose not to obey or don't care if we
obey, it's because His word is not in our heart; it's in our
mind and our mind needs to be changed and that can only
happen when we study the Bible.

> And be not conformed to this world: but be ye
> transformed by the renewing of your mind,

that ye may prove what is that good, and
acceptable, and perfect, will of God.—
Romans 12:2

God gave Moses the Ten Commandments and in that
time in history it was still being prophesied that Messiah
would come, and so the Holy Spirit had not yet been given to
believers. Back then, they actually had to believe without the
inspiration of the Holy Spirit, but now, believers are filled
with His Spirit who convicts us of sin. The commandments
that God gave to Moses are no longer rules that we have to
obey; they are written in our heart and we want to obey.

> 'For this is the covenant that I will make with
> the house of Israel after those days,' saith the
> Lord; 'I will put my laws into their mind, and
> write them in their hearts: and I will be to
> them a God, and they shall be to me a
> people.'—Hebrews 8:10

Many so-called-Christians continue to live in sin
because they either don't read the Bible to know it's wrong
or they don't want to change. They don't have a relationship
with Jesus and don't study the Bible with a heart to know
Him. People who don't obey God's word because their
church doesn't teach it cannot use that as an excuse when
they face the Lord on Judgment Day.

False doctrines don't teach the truth of the Bible—
that's why they're false. They teach a congenial message that
will keep the people coming, the church popular and the
leaders prosperous. Obeying God is not necessary to them;
following them is what's important. The devil wants to keep
people from knowing the truth so he's provided a deception
where they think they are "Christians" without having to be
committed or obedient to God.

> For the time will come when they will not
> endure sound doctrine; but after their own
> lusts shall they heap to themselves teachers,
> having itching ears.—2 Timothy 4:3

Romans 6:23 tells us that the wages of sin is death, so when we willfully continue to live in sin and disobey God, then we have to realize that we will pay the punishment for our sins when we stand before God and get judged by the very law that we chose to disobey.

> Know ye not, that to whom ye yield
> yourselves servants to obey, his servants ye
> are to whom ye obey; whether of sin unto
> death, or of obedience unto righteousness?—
> Romans 6:16

Love is not Silent

Many Christians do not share the gospel of Jesus with others because they feel "shy" and just don't have the words to say. Others believe that if they talk about it then they may appear to be judging others by telling them that they have sin in their life. Yet, we're not judging anyone when we are sharing the gospel with them, or when we point out blatant sins in their lives that will keep them from God. The truth is, God's children need to speak out and share the gospel because love is not silent!

If there was a hole in the road up ahead and we knew that a car full of children was heading toward it unknowingly, wouldn't we want to warn the driver of the danger up ahead? Wouldn't our heart be afraid for those people knowing that they will all die if they keep going? Out of sheer love for people, we surely would want to warn them. It would be wrong to do nothing, to say it's not our problem because it is our problem. We know of the danger and we should to warn them because they don't know.

How guilty we would feel when we learned of their death—one that could have been prevented if we'd warned them! And likewise, how guilty we'll be when we know that others are headed to hell because we didn't consider it our duty to warn them!

> When I say unto the wicked, 'Thou shalt surely die; and thou givest him not warning, nor speakest to warn the wicked from his wicked way, to save his life; the same wicked man shall die in his iniquity; but his blood will I require at thine hand'.—Ezekiel 3:18

The only thing that separates us from God is sin. We were all born with sin because we are all ancestors of Adam and Eve who turned their backs on God and brought sin upon us all. God withdrew His Spirit from them because of this sin and they became the sole possessions of the devil, the epitome of sin. But because God loved them so much and because sin cannot stand in His presence without being burned up, He could no longer dwell with them. But He did not forget them; He promised to send them a Savior who would bring us all back to Him.

As Christians, we know the love of God and the salvation of Jesus. But there are many "good" people in the world who are content thinking that God is okay with them because, after all, they've never really broken any of the main commandments. They haven't killed anyone, don't have graven images in their home and haven't robbed a bank, so they're okay. But unfortunately, even one tiny sin—one seemingly unimportant little lie committed sometime during their life—is still sin! And it will find them guilty and they will be sentenced to eternal hell when they die because the law will convict them for it.

> For the wages of sin is death; but the gift of God is eternal life through Jesus Christ our Lord.—Romans 6:23

It is our responsibility to help the lost find Jesus, and not only that, but it's what we do in obedience to God. This commission isn't the job of just pastors or preachers; it's the job of every single Christian! The pastor's job is to build the congregation up so they can stay spiritually strong to go out into the mission field and bring the lost to Jesus, and so they can pray for the sick and help those who need help. Jesus told us all to preach the gospel.

> And He said unto them, 'Go ye into all the world, and preach the gospel to every creature'.—Mark 16:15

We don't have to be aggressive or rude or judgmental when we tell others about the Lord. In fact, the best way to know that we are witnessing to others in a good attitude is to pray and study the scriptures so we can not only learn about God, but so we can know His love is in us. When we are confident of God's love, we are able to share that love with others. We can talk to the lost and tell them about Jesus in a loving way. We can't just walk up to someone and tell them that they're a sinner going to hell because that person will think we're rude and judgemental and won't talk to us. Jesus didn't approach people that way and neither should we.

We need to engage in conversations with people and meet them at their level so we can communicate with them and bring them up to God's level. No, we don't agree with them or participate in worldly sins with them, but we can talk to them with an attitude of love and understanding so we can win their confidence. Our own actions and caring attitude will allow us the opportunity to talk about their sins and then we can share the gospel with them. And we do that without calling them names or judging them. We can show them God's love and tell them that if they're not saved they'll stand to be judged for their sin when they die, but that if they repent and accept Jesus now they will live forever with Him in Heaven.

> How then shall they call on Him in whom they have not believed? And how shall they believe in Him of whom they have not heard? And how shall they hear without a preacher?—Romans 10:14

We have to warn people that Judgment Day is coming! We have to tell them that anyone who has not accepted Jesus as their Savior and who has not repented of their sins and been pardoned by Him will be judged by the law for those sins—and the punishment comes without parole. It's eternity in hell and no movie on this earth has come close to the horror and fear of that judgment.

Jesus is soon to return as King to rule over the whole world, but right before that He will pour out His wrath upon this sinful world, and it's known as The Great Tribulation—Daniel 12, Matthew 24:21. It will be a time of evil and hardship that this world has never seen before and will never see again. We need to warn people that it's coming and show them that Jesus has provided a means of salvation whereby they can escape it.

Let's not keep God's love to our self. Let's share that love with the lost so they can be saved and know Jesus. Let's get out there and do God's will and warn them while there's still time. When we get to Heaven, we want God to be happy with us and not disappointed because we didn't warn the people that He put across our path. We can't say that His love is in us when we don't share it with others. We will be accountable for our actions—or lack of—because it is wrong to stay silent and hide God's love from people. It's wrong to not care that someone could have made it to Heaven if we'd only cared enough to tell them about it.

> His lord said unto him, 'Well done, thou good and faithful servant: thou hast been faithful over a few things, I will make thee ruler over many things: enter thou into the joy of thy lord.'—Matthew 25:21

We need to be God's disciples and we need to share His love with others and tell them about Heaven and hell so they can realize that there is a choice to make. To not say anything to them and to just leave them to live in their sin would show a lack of love on our part. And if God's love for us can take Jesus to the cross to be crucified, then surely our love for God can tell others that He did it!

112

Beloved, let us love one another: for love is of God; and every one that loveth is born of God, and knoweth God. 8 He that loveth not knoweth not God; for God is love. 9 In this was manifested the love of God toward us, because that God sent his only begotten Son into the world, that we might live through him. 10 Herein is love, not that we loved God, but that He loved us, and sent His Son to be the propitiation for our sins. 11 Beloved, if God so loved us, we ought also to love one another.—1 John 4:7-11

Are Old Testament Laws for Today?

The Tablets that God gave to Moses were God's law carved by His own hand, and it was for all of mankind; a standard of living that ruled over the people so they could know the difference between right and wrong. But God's laws are being greatly challenged today. Much of the so-called "church" is modifying His laws to meet with their own modern-day lifestyles, and the world is changing the laws so that the abnormal can become the norm. So, with these two entities wanting change to meet their own selfish lusts, they can't agree fast enough that God's Old Testament Laws are not for today.

We're told in Genesis 1:1 that God is the creator of the Universe. We learn in Hebrews 13:8 that Jesus (who is the Son of God) is the same yesterday, today and forever. Deuteronomy 32:4 tells us that, "He is the Rock, His work is perfect: for all His ways are judgment: a God of truth and without iniquity, just and right is He." And 1 John 3:20 tells us that He sees and knows everything. God gave these laws and then issued judgments and punishments to the people of the Old Testament times who sinned against His laws without coming to Him and asking for forgiveness. He reminds us throughout the New Testament of how serious His laws are and of the need to become born again so we no longer have to be under the judgment of His law, but rather, under His forgiveness and grace.

Therefore, it is not God's will to have one word of His law changed. It is wrong for anyone to flagrantly change His laws to suit their own lusts and desires.

> For verily I say unto you, Till heaven and earth pass, one jot or one tittle shall in no wise pass from the law, till all be fulfilled.— Matthew 5:18

God is not a harsh, selfish ruler who demands our love and wants things to be done His way or else! But rather, He is a loving Father who knows what lengths the devil will go to in order to destroy us, His children. And so He made laws for His children to follow so that they would know the difference between right and wrong and not get lured into the corruption of sin. God's laws were and still are the benchmark by which all people are to guide their lives.

Yet, today we have changed many of the laws to suit the sinful hearts of man, and look where we are now!

Thou shalt have no other gods before me:— Exodus 20:3

God made it law in the Old Testament that His children should worship only Him as their God, and He did this so they would obey Him and not fall into the sin of serving other gods that all lead to death. Yet today, through the freedom of religion, we are flooded with churches that worship and give glory to a false god, the devil. And the government has allowed them to be official "churches of worship. So God's law has been changed and the sin of idolatry is now widely accepted AND legal throughout our land. All religions are welcome to build their own churches and worship their own gods; a blatant defiance of idolatry!

Thou shalt not take the name of the Lord thy God in vain:—Exodus 20:7

There used to be a sense of guilt, shame and embarrassment to hear someone use the Lord's name as a swear word, and it was considered blasphemy to even jest or hint at mocking His name. But today, the name of Jesus—the name above all names—is not only a swear word, but has become the centre of many cynical and disgusting jokes.

People have become so used to this sin that they don't even bow in shame anymore.

> Remember the sabbath day, to keep it holy:—
> Exodus 20:8

Years ago, Sunday's were quiet days, and although this isn't the official Jewish Sabbath, it is the day that Christians set aside to worship the Lord. People went to church, and stores and businesses were closed. There was an understanding and a respect given to God on this day. However, the laws have changed so that Sunday's (or Sabbath days) are just like any other day; all businesses are open (including bars) and there is no special reverence given to the day. It is just another day, which also forces people to work instead of being free to spend time with the Lord.

> Thou shalt not kill:—Exodus 20:13

Years ago the punishment for killing anyone was so heavy that the people feared the thoughts of killing anyone, especially a minister of the gospel, police officers, children or disabled people! But the "absolute law" has been modified so that the punishment is not nearly as greatly feared as used to be. As a result, we have drive-by shootings and mass killings that take dozens of lives far too often because the fear of punishment is not there. And if that isn't bad enough, our law makers have legalized the process of abortion so that hundreds and thousands of unborn babies are being brutally and horrifically murdered every day! The law has been changed so that THESE MURDERS ARE LEGAL!

> Thou shalt not commit adultery:—Exodus 20:14

In Bible times when people were caught in the act of adultery, they were stoned to death. There was no allowance for this sin. Then, because Moses knew that the people would

116

only delve into adultery if they couldn't get out of a bad marriage, he asked God to allow them to divorce under certain circumstances. But today, the law has changed so that marriage isn't even necessary for two people to live intimately together. In fact, it's legally recognized as a real relationship, regardless if one or both is already married to someone else or not. And not only is this sin legal, but now the gays and lesbians can also live together as a married couple AND receive all the same legal and financial benefits. God's law has not only been changed to promote adultery, but also to flaunt an abomination before God, as well.

Changing these laws has not only angered God because He said not to change anything that He'd written in the scriptures for us—Revelations 22:18 & 19— but it has drawn humanity away from God and down a corrupt and sinful path that is heading for hell. There is good reason why God doesn't want His laws changed, and we can see why by just looking at the world around us and comparing it to what it was just a few years ago.

In Old Testament days, the people were ruled by kings and judges who sought God's counsel daily through the prophets. Yes, government and "religion" were one. But today, the people don't want God or anything that relates to Him in their government—another bad change! They want to keep the church and the government separate so that God's laws don't prevail.

Jesus told us clearly that His law would not change. The salvation He provided whereby we are forgiven for our sins does not eliminate any part of His law. We are no longer judged by them on Judgment Day, but that is because we are able to repent from our sins and through His grace we are forgiven. But we are still expected to follow His laws. Jesus didn't change the law when He came; He fulfilled it.

117

> Think not that I am come to destroy the law,
> or the prophets: I am not come to destroy, but
> to fulfil.—Matthew 5:17

The Laws of God are the same today as they were the day they were given. They are not up for change because the people have drifted from God and don't feel convicted by His laws any more. They will stand before God one day and be judged by the law for every single time they sinned, just as a criminal is judged by our earthly law today. And as we know, the wages of sin is death—Romans 6:23. We need to study the scriptures and learn them so that we can obey Him and truly can represent God in everything we do.

> This book of the law shall not depart out of
> thy mouth; but thou shalt meditate therein day
> and night, that thou mayest observe to do
> according to all that is written therein: for
> then thou shalt make thy way prosperous, and
> then thou shalt have good success.—Joshua
> 1:8

God was very clear that the law He gave to Moses on those tablets would not end or pass away until the end of time. And time is still going so we need to obey God.

> For there is no respect of persons with God.
> 12 For as many as have sinned without law
> shall also perish without law: and as many as
> have sinned in the law shall be judged by the
> law.—Romans 2:11-12

The Hope of Heaven is Fading

We know Reverend Billy Graham as the renowned figure on television who has preached a powerful gospel message around the globe for over 50 years. Many of us have had the opportunity to attend one of his crusades and the impact of his message still ministers to us today. God has used this man to preach the gospel and call people to repentance, and even in his later years Rev. Graham has continued to tell people about Christ and the hope of Heaven that God has given to those who love Him. If this precious, aged man can still share messages of hope with the world, then surely we can follow his example and tell those around us of the hope God has given to those who love Him.

God provided our salvation through His own shed blood on the cross so that we could be forgiven for our sins and live with Him in Heaven forever. And while we're here on earth, it is our commission from Him to spread the good news to others because we are now the light of the world and God is revealed through us.

> Then spake Jesus again unto them, saying, 'I am the light of the world: he that followeth me shall not walk in darkness, but shall have the light of life'.—John 8:12

> ...and Jesus continued...

> Ye are the light of the world. A city that is set on an hill cannot be hid. 15 Neither do men light a candle, and put it under a bushel, but on a candlestick; and it giveth light unto all that are in the house. 16 Let your light so shine before men, that they may see your good works, and glorify your Father which is in heaven.—Matthew 5:14-16

Unfortunately, many of us have become so caught up with our own personal lives that we've actually fallen into the "modus operandi" or process of this world's system and don't even realize it. We have our families, jobs and careers that have become our main priorities and we literally live our lives for them and only include God when we remember. And while it's good that we diligently provide for our families and better ourselves, these priorities should never become our reason for living. They should never come before our love for Jesus or before His commission for us here on earth. And the treasures we value should never be greater than the treasures that God has waiting for us in Heaven.

It's hard to even imagine how wonderful Heaven really is, and it's difficult to put the description of the New Jerusalem into our thoughts realistically because it is so magnificent. The Bible tells that there are mansions in Heaven and that He created them for each of us personally. This isn't mass production of same style townhomes; each mansion is designed uniquely for each of His children.

> In my Father's house are many mansions: if it were not so, I would have told you. I go to prepare a place for you.—John 14:2

Jesus says that there is peace in Heaven; no more pain and no more tears. How wonderful it will be to never feel sorrow, to never experience hurt or pain again, and to never cry from sadness because there will be no sadness there.

> And God shall wipe away all tears from their eyes; and there shall be no more death, neither sorrow, nor crying, neither shall there be any more pain: for the former things are passed away.—Revelation 21:4

The lion will lay down with the lamb and children will be carefree and happy. No more worries about strangers; no more fear for their health. Just peace and safety!

> The wolf and the lamb shall feed together, and the lion shall eat straw like the bullock: and dust shall be the serpent's meat. They shall not hurt nor destroy in all my holy mountain, saith the Lord.—Isaiah 65:25

And while all of these things make Heaven so inviting, the most wonderful part of it is that Jesus is there! The Bible says that we will be with Jesus throughout eternity, so wherever He is, we will also be—and this is our greatest hope for Heaven. This is the reason we live!

> ...that where I am, there ye may be also.—John 14:3

Heaven has no boundaries and its size is beyond our imagination— and yet, there is only ONE door to get in. And that door is Jesus Christ.

> I am the door: by me if any man enter in, he shall be saved, and shall go in and out, and find pasture.—John 10:9

The future that awaits those who don't invite Him into their hearts and who don't accept the salvation that Jesus provided on the cross for them, is one of complete separation from God. The Bible says in Matthew 8:12 and in Matthew 22:13 that they will be cast out into outer darkness.

According to STRONGS Concordance NT 1857, the Greek words for "outer darkness" are (ἐξώτερος) exóteros and (σκότος) skotos. Thayer's Greek Lexicon says that exóteros means "the darkness outside the limits of the lighted palace (to which the Messiah's kingdom is here likened)", and that skotos means "By metonymy, put for a dark place."

The Bible often refers to hell as a pit, a low place, a dark place—outer darkness—and it's a place where God's holiness does not reside even though it's within his purview because He is omnipresent. No person, if they had even a glimpse of what hell really is, would want to reside there because hell is a place of punishment, and after the great Judgment Day, death and hell will both be cast into the Lake of Fire. And this is what the Bible refers to as the second death, where all those who are in them will burn forever.

> And death and hell were cast into the lake of fire. This is the second death.—Revelation 20:14

We learn in John 3:16 that it is not God's will that any of us should perish. He made people because He wanted a family, and when sin entered into Adam that family relationship was destroyed. But God has never given up on us. He came to earth and lived as a man so that He alone could take that sin and put it into hell where it and anyone found with sin would wait for judgment. And He did it so that we would not have to go there.

Our Heavenly Father has never stopped loving us, and when we accept the salvation that Jesus gave on the cross, we are free of that sin. And then He will come and live in us and be with us until we go Home to Heaven and live forever more.

Unfortunately, some people think that a loving God could not send anyone to hell. They believe that everyone is saved because it says in Romans 14:11 that every knee shall bow to the name of Jesus. Yes, every knee shall bow, but that's because there's nothing else anyone can do in the presence of Almighty God except fall to their knees and worship Him. Whether a person believes now that Jesus is real or not doesn't change the fact that when they die they'll stand before Him and they will know then that He is God ..... AND THEY WILL BOW!

Jesus is our Lord, our Savior and our King! And one day He will return to rule over the entire earth whether people want to accept that fact or not. Too many people push Him away or plan to make it right later on in life. But, there is no guarantee that any of us has a "later on in life" waiting for us. The time to accept our salvation is now!

The opportunity to know Jesus is now. The time to repent is now. The time to turn away from the world and follow Jesus is NOW! Jesus wants YOU to be there with Him in Heaven forever!

> The Lord is not slack concerning his promise, as some men count slackness; but is longsuffering to us-ward, not willing that any should perish, but that all should come to repentance.—2 Peter 3:9

Pride that Separates us from God

There are two kinds of pride that can keep us away from God. Most Christians won't even realize that they are guilty of one or the other, but when we review the scripture that says we all sin and fall short of the glory of God, we'll all likely see that we have been guilty of one of these at some point in our Christian walk. Perhaps it didn't seem significant at the time, but it's something that if it's left to grow, can change our attitude and separate us from God.

I can do it myself!

Many Christians have the attitude that they can work out their problems on their own and that they are not going to bother God with them. Some say that God is too busy taking care of the disasters of the world to have to stop and help people with little problems. Others say that He expects people to do all they can do first, and He will do the rest when they don't succeed. Yet, nowhere in the Bible does Jesus even suggest this. In fact, He tells us to cast all of our burdens onto Him. Not just the little ones, but ALL of our burdens.

> Casting all your care upon Him; for He careth
> for you.—1 Peter 5:7

Too often, we won't turn to God for help because we don't want to bother Him with small issues. We feel it's better to only ask Him to help with the big things; after all, we are intelligent beings who like to take care of ourselves. This is called "pride" and it will destroy anyone who believes it! It will smother our faith in God and even ruin our relationship with Him because we refuse to submit our whole life over to Him.

> Pride goeth before destruction, and an
> haughty spirit before a fall.—Proverbs 16:18

We read in Luke 19:10, "For the Son of man is come to seek and to save that which was lost." Jesus would not have come down from Heaven to sacrifice His life and save our souls if our lives were not worth it to Him. He takes interest in every aspect and not just with the big problems that are too great for us to handle on our own. He came not only to save us from sin, but to bring us into His family. Right now we live in a world that is ruled by the devil—and this is evident in the lawlessness and immorality that surrounds us. But Jesus came and defeated the devil so that those who would accept Him could live freely in Him.

This world is being swallowed up with evil and if we think that we can fight the devil and win on our own merits, then we are deceiving ourselves and we will fail. When we have any problems at all, we need to take them to the Lord because only HE can win over the devil. Jesus went to the cross and gave us the victory over sin and death. Let's not be so foolish as to think that we don't need God in every minute of our lives while we're here on earth—because we do! Because for every one of those minutes that we're here, that devil is going to come against us with one thing or another. It won't stop until we're home with Jesus. So let's call upon Him with all of our needs.

> These things I have spoken unto you, that in me ye might have peace. In the world ye shall have tribulation: but be of good cheer; I have overcome the world.—John 16:33

Many Christians don't take their problems to the Lord because they don't really have a relationship with Him. They feel that He is "God" in Heaven that they'll meet one day, and they go to church and that's where they leave it. But, this is not a relationship with Jesus; this is just doing works that mean nothing to God. Jesus wants us to be part of Him. He says in Revelation 3:20, "Behold, I stand at the door, and

125

knock: if any man hear my voice, and open the door, I will come in to him, and will sup with him, and he with me." What a wonderful promise!

The Puffed-up Christian!

On the flip side of this issue is pride that many Christians carry when they feel that they have arrived at perfection. They think that because they've been saved for years, attended church, paid tithes, and supported the local missionaries that they are better than the rest of us. They are financially well off and live very modest lives, and because they have some knowledge of the scriptures, they are just better Christians than most.

And while this attitude is anything but Christian because we are to be humble and ready to give an answer at any time for the joy of the Lord that's in us—1 Peter 3:15—, it's an attitude that raises itself up to a dangerous height. This is what Satan did; he felt that he was better than the rest of the angels and no longer needed to be humble before God, but instead, demanded to be respected and honored by those around him. It was his intention to take their allegiance from God and draw it onto himself. This attitude leads to destruction!

It's a pride that truly comes before a fall because it literally replaces our submission, dependence, reverence, and love to the Lord. This attitude doesn't show the love of God in us, but instead, it blocks any rays of love from the heart towards others, and from others toward us. God has told us to love the brethren as much as we love God because it's His love in us that shows love to others. And when we are too proud to receive advice or love from the brethren, we fall into the pride that brings destruction. And if this attitude isn't changed, it could be the thing that leads to a mighty fall.

The Pharisee stood and prayed thus with himself, 'God, I thank You that I am not like other men—extortioners, unjust, adulterers, or even as this tax collector.' ....14(Jesus said) I tell you, this man went down to his house justified rather than the other; for everyone who exalts himself will be humbled, and he who humbles himself will be exalted.".— Luke 18:11, 14 NKJV

Pride opposes a personal relationship with the Lord!

Being a Christian means following Jesus and knowing Him personally. It means studying the Bible and learning all about God and who we are in Christ. Jesus is the Son of God, the one who sacrificed His life on the cross to pay for our sins so that we wouldn't have to stand before God on Judgment Day and be judged because of the sin in us. This is not just a nice thing that He did. This is a GREAT thing that Jesus did! He died for us because He loves us, and He is worthy of our praises every minute of every day!

Jesus wants to have a relationship with us here on earth and He hears every single prayer that we pray when we become born again—aka Christians. But many think that He only answers big requests, and some feel they are mature Christians and don't need to ask for His help. Where is the relationship? If we would all study the scriptures and get to know God, we would become more humble in His presence. There is no father on earth who loves his children more than our Heavenly Father loves us, and He loves it when we talk to Him. And He wants to hear everything!

Now we know that God heareth not sinners: but if any man be a worshipper of God, and doeth His will, him He heareth.—John 9:31

When we see God as our Heavenly Father who loves us, and when we see ourselves as His beloved children, we will want to talk to Him about everything and anything. We won't feel that we are inferior, and we won't feel puffed up. We will know His love and submit to Him, and we will be free to give Him all the glory that He deserves!

> Humble yourselves therefore under the mighty hand of God, that he may exalt you in due time.—1 Peter 5:6

Pride that Kills

There is another kind of pride that also destroys and it is the cause of many people being hurt and even ruined. It's buried deep under an anguish of pain and anger that's caused from a disability and it brings resentment and torment. Those affected take great offense to any remarks or suggestions given to them as they try to cover the pain and embarrassment of needing help. They don't see someone offering their hand as a deed of kindness, but as an act of ridicule. And they see their disability as a punishment or test from God and they don't feel His divine presence. But He is there, and yet, the anguish caused by their disability steals their joy and their ability to see Him!

Many handicapped people develop an attitude of resentment toward others because they are not able to do the things that they once did, or that they want to do for themselves. Maybe it's a physical disability, a financial hardship or a hurt from the past that has left them broken. They are disappointed in themselves and feel like a complete failure because they cannot be independent. So when someone comes to them and wants to help, their back gets up and they see it as another attack against their already deplored ego. Their heart becomes colder as their need to be self-sufficient—driven by their pride—grows stronger. They ignore their own cry for help and let their pride rule.

> A man's pride shall bring him low: but honour shall uphold the humble in spirit.—Proverbs 29:23

It's an attitude of pride that will keep them from God and not allow them to see His goodness through others. It steals their joy and separates them from their Heavenly Father who wants to help them. Sometimes the issues that torment them bring them shame and make them feel as if they're not worthy to be helped. Or on the flip side, they're angry that they have been afflicted and see the help of others as pity—which adds to their humiliation. They can't see—or don't want to see—that God is sending people to help them. They are blinded to their own situation, a tactic of the devil that slowly kills their joy and makes them feel unwanted.

> The thief cometh not, but for to steal, and to kill, and to destroy: I am come that they might have life, and that they might have it more abundantly.—John 10:10

Every good thing that comes to us comes from God, and every bad thing that comes against us comes from the devil. But the devil does not have authority over our lives and anything that he gives to us must be first be approved by God. And God will not allow anything that we cannot handle. So when we find ourselves in a position where we can't do the things we want to do we cannot just give in and give the devil glory by accepting defeat and getting angry. We need to pray about it. We need to seek God and find out why He has allowed this, and what He wants us to do about it.

> And we know that all things work together for good to them that love God, to them who are the called according to his purpose.—Romans 8:28

When we're afflicted with an issue that can literally change our life we need to come to God and ask Him why. We need to come with an open heart that is willing to listen AND to obey. We need to ask Him to forgive us for our anger and hostility toward Him and toward our brethren that has been brought on by our frustration, and we need to ditch the pride from anger that has caused us to be ungrateful.

Sometimes God just wants to pull us away from the world that we've been slowly drifting back into. Sometimes He has a job for us to do and He knows that this is the only way to get our attention. Regardless of the reason, we need to seek God with a humble heart. Nothing is impossible to God and He can make our situation right in a second, but we need to trust Him. And we need to take our eyes off of what we can't do on our own, and put them onto God who will give us the strength to move mountains.

> Trust in the Lord with all thine heart; and lean not unto thine own understanding.—Proverbs 3:5

If we take on the attitude that people around us aren't friendly and just assume it's because of our disability, then we are already heading in the wrong direction. We reap what we sow—disabled or not—and if we want people to be friendly to us, then we need to be friendly toward them. Perhaps instead of turning people away when they try to help, we could find the goodness in their gesture and see the compassion of their actions and not refuse the hand of God that's been stretched out to us.

> A man who has friends must himself be friendly.—Proverbs 18:24

The ones who are willing to help and who offer their love are not perfect, either. Many of them are enduring their own hardships and sorrows, but they have learned to give them to God so they can be a blessing to others. We need to see the goodness in people and thank God that He has sent them out to help those in need, and not allow the devil to steal the joy of the Lord from us or from them.

There will be those out there who are judgmental and overbearing, rude and talk with a motor-mouth that's filled

131

with condemnation towards those who suffer with disabilities. They don't serve the Lord, don't appreciate His value for life and have allowed their own selfish thoughts to hurt others. But these are not sent from God and we shouldn't let them get us down. We are Christians. So let's focus on the things of God and give Him glory.

> Finally, brethren, whatsoever things are true, whatsoever things are honest, whatsoever things are just, whatsoever things are pure, whatsoever things are lovely, whatsoever things are of good report; if there be any virtue, and if there be any praise, think on these things.—Philippians 4:8

As children in the family of God, we need to help each other because we all live in a world that is headed for destruction and we cannot be an island unto ourselves. It's too lonely and painful on that island. We need each other. We need to see each other as kin and lift each other up, help where we can, give when it's available and love at all times. Then we truly will be free of the hurts that have got us down and that are trying to destroy us. Then we will see that when others offer to help, they are doing it in love.

Then the pride and anger that once kept us in bondage will be gone, and we will be as free and loving as any Christian can be. God may even heal us so that we no longer bear the disability, but because of it we will have a better understanding of how others feel and of what they are going through and it will enable us to be a greater witness to them. Whether we get our healing or not, our heart will still be pure and it will overflow with a love for God and for our brethren. We will be able to do the job that God has called us to do and He will give us the ability to do it well.

Our physical disability may never leave us, but our attitude, our appreciation for what God has given to us, and our love for God will be changed when we surrender it all to Him. We will no longer be angry or critical towards others because we'll be free from the hurts that have tormented us and stopped us from loving them. Our lives will become a great witness and we may have a more significant impact on others because of our disability, and all to the glory of God.

Blessed are the pure in heart: for they shall see God.—Matthew 5:8

Dancing Shoes

The internet has made it possible for us to spend less time doing those tedious things such as banking, shopping and travelling to work, giving us more time to do what we like to do. Unfortunately, this "convenience" has also spread into the Christian life so that many have adopted a lazy attitude towards God. They rely on teachers and preachers to get them into Heaven instead of seeking God themselves. There is only one way that we'll ever know God and that is to study the Bible and let God's Holy Spirit bring it to life! So let's come alive and put on our dancing shoes!

The Bible IS life and as we study it to truly learn about God, the patriarchs and the Bible stories all come alive! As we read the Bible over and over prayerfully, things begin to fall into place and it's no longer just a book of instruction and history, but it becomes our own personal chronicle of ancestry events. It comes alive and we slowly become part of it!

> But whosoever drinketh of the water that I shall give him shall never thirst; but the water that I shall give him shall be in him a well of water springing up into everlasting life.— John 4:14

We begin to understand our Heavenly Father as we realize the depth of evil and rebellion that He has had to deal with over the years. We learn in the Old Testament how so many people chose to disobey Him and live wicked, corrupt and evil lives. They worshipped idols and false gods, chased after their own lusts and even brutally murdered and sacrificed their own children to these gods. Nations as a whole were led by evil leaders who encouraged the people to turn from obeying Yeshua so they could worship false gods. Through it all we can feel God's pain and we can understand

His anger toward those who deliberately turned their backs on Him to follow pagan gods into a life of eternal punishment.

> He that believeth on the Son hath everlasting life: and he that believeth not the Son shall not see life; but the wrath of God abideth on him.—John 3:36

And here we are in the modern-day world and people haven't changed at all. In fact, it may even be worse now only not as blatantly noticeable because people have learned to live discretely. God is still being rejected by majority of the world as it thrives on a modern-day version of that same ancient, ungodly and barbaric lifestyle. And we can see these sins clearly in the growing immorality around us, not to mention the millions of unborn babies being sacrificed daily to the god of self or pleasure.

And through this same modernization of an "easy life", many Christians have become too dependent on others to teach them about God while they spend their time enjoying life. Since few of these so-called "Christians" actually read or study the Bible to know the truth, they just assume that the doctrine they've chosen to follow is the right one. After all, it suits all of their needs; it allows them to live the lifestyle they choose, gain all the riches they can and sin without repentance since they believe that everyone is saved. And they don't need to seek after God for themselves because the preacher has a special rapport with God who tells him about all the changes He's made for this time we're living in.

But God has NOT changed to suit this modern world and people need to realize that any preacher who says that He has changed is a false preacher. We are living in the last hour before Christ returns as king to rule the entire world, and if we'll study the Bible we'll know all about that. We'll also know when the preachers are speaking truth and when they're preaching a false doctrine because we'll know the scriptures and we'll know the truth.

The only way any of us will know God is to study the scriptures ourselves, pray to the Lord as a submissive and grateful child, and worship Him with all of our heart, soul, mind and strength. Then we'll know that we know God and we'll know what is right and what is wrong because we'll have the wisdom of God in us—wisdom and knowledge that we learn by instruction from Him as we read the Bible. We won't be fooled by false teaching.

> Study to shew thyself approved unto God, a workman that needeth not to be ashamed, rightly dividing the word of truth.—2 Timothy 2:15

Christians, especially new ones, have a million questions because the different rules and standards of the many doctrines that surround us are confusing and they make God sound as if He does change with the times. And they don't know which one to follow. The only way to get God's answer is to study the Bible and know what He says. We need the truth revealed to us by God's Holy Spirit as we study the scriptures. Any person on their own and through their own understanding will never be able to know the truth, only their own interpretation of what they think is truth according to what they want it to mean.

This author has written a book called, "NO COMPROMISE! *Biblical Answers to Some of Today's Issues",* and it's filled with questions that many Christians have concerning some of the issues that affect them today. The answers are scriptures only—no opinions or bias. Yet, even though it was written so that readers can know what God has said, they need to study the Bible themselves to confirm the answers. We must always check the scriptures to prove what is truth, and through this diligence the Spirit of God will reveal the truth into our heart!

> And the brethren immediately sent away Paul and Silas by night unto Berea: who coming thither went into the synagogue of the Jews. 11 These were more noble than those in Thessalonica, in that they received the word with all readiness of mind, and searched the scriptures daily, whether those things were so.—Acts 17:10-11

It's really important that each of us knows God personally, and not just know of Him. When we leave this earth, we want to be sure where we're going—not hope that we're going Heaven, but know that we're going to Heaven. There's no second chance given once we leave. Contrary to the New Age religion, God doesn't give us one last opportunity to accept Him as Lord when we stand before Him at the Great White Throne. Every knee will bow to Him, and that's because He is God and every person will bow to Him whether they knew Him before or just learn it then. Now is all the time we have to accept Christ and be saved from God's wrath that will come to all that is sin. Let's study the Bible and know God! Let's grab our dancing shoes because the Bible will come to life and the truth will be in us and we'll be praising God and dancing our way to Heaven!

> The thief cometh not, but for to steal, and to kill, and to destroy: I am come that they might have life, and that they might have it more abundantly.—John 10:10

Sowing Discord

Much of today's so-called Christian community has deviated from the real gospel of Jesus to serve many man-made doctrines and ideals. One of the greatest deceptions to circulate the globe is the idea that we are all one in Christ regardless of how much of the Bible we choose to believe, how we elect to interpret it, or who our god is. Unfortunately, this has caused many to drift far from the truth in their endeavor to "do it their way", and many are no longer even Christians; they just think they are. And it all began when discord was sown in the church and was allowed to grow.

When we go back to the early church that began on the day of Pentecost, we see that the people had one thing in common: they all loved Jesus. Not themselves. Not a reasonable facsimile of the gospel, but only the gospel. Acts 2:1 says, "And when the day of Pentecost was fully come, they were all with one accord in one place." One accord! There was no division among them even though they came from different backgrounds and traditions. They were all willing to give up what they'd been trained in so they could follow Jesus and His gospel. They had no intention of allowing their personal cultures or differences to overrule their love for God and their obedience to Him.

There was one message preached that day and it was the gospel of Jesus Christ. Peter stood boldly and preached a powerful sermon to the Jews and to other nationalities, and that message brought over 3,000 people to Christ that day. These people repented, turned from their old beliefs and followed the teaching of Jesus, even though they came from a wide range of backgrounds and had different jobs, interests and mannerisms. We know that there were at least fifteen different cultures of people who attended that first Christian service because their languages are mentioned in verses 8-11.

Peter preached one message to everyone! He did not regard culture or tradition and had no intentions of trying to please any of them. In Acts chapter two, he told them who Christ was and then explained clearly that in order to be a Christian they must repent of their sins, turn from the world of sin and follow Jesus so they could be born-again and filled with His Spirit. He didn't add in any personal opinions or suggestions—and none of his own interpretations; he just told them what Jesus said.

> Then Peter said unto them, 'Repent, and be baptized every one of you in the name of Jesus Christ for the remission of sins, and ye shall receive the gift of the Holy Ghost'.— Acts 2:38

Verse 41 says that they were all baptized and followed Jesus and His gospel. We read on in verses 44 and 45 that they had all things in common and that some sold their possessions to ensure that no one lacked anything. Nowhere does it say that they all had to eat certain foods, or dress in a particular fashion or give money to get rich. It says they had all things in common and looked after each other in spite of the fact that they came from different backgrounds because now they were no longer separated by nationalities, but rather, they were one in Christ.

Unfortunately, as time went on, Christians would not remain "in one accord", and God warned the new believers through Apostle Paul that things would not always be so simple. He told them that soon wolves would come into the flock and corrupt the truth with discord. He encouraged the believers to stay in the scriptures, to stick together and to follow only the teaching of Jesus—and to turn from anyone who did not teach the full gospel of Christ.

> For I know this, that after my departing shall grievous wolves enter in among you, not sparing the flock. 30 Also of your own selves shall men arise, speaking perverse things, to draw away disciples after them.—Acts 20:29-30

There is discord being sown in the body of the church today and it's deceiving the people and tearing God's children away from His church family. It's amazing how the world can come against the church and immediately it can see it coming and prepare to defend itself, yet it's blind to the discord that's being sown right inside its own walls.

Today we have dozens of issues that have not been resolved by using the scriptures as a benchmark. But rather, they have been settled by simply creating a new variation of the doctrine of Christ and then establishing another congregation of people who can be "Christians" under their own terms. Everyone is happy and they all feel that they still belong to God. But they have drifted from God to serve themselves. They foolishly believe that they can come to God their way, serve Him their way and still be saved and headed toward Heaven. Did they learn nothing from Cain and Abel when Cain tried to serve God his way?—Genesis 4:1-16

There is a big difference between accepting personal differences and interests among the brethren, and accepting new and diverse gospels. Children within a family may have different personalities and personal interests, but they all honor the parents and obey them. And they'll defend their brothers and sisters regardless of their differences because they are family. They are bonded and knitted together with love, just as the Christian family is knitted together by the love of God and their obedience to HIS gospel.

And yet, the church is being torn apart by internal discord. Instead of standing fast for Christ alone, the church family is watching some of its members separate and do things their own way. The Bible warns us in Mark 3:25 that a house divided will fall. And so as a result, we have hundreds of manmade doctrines—that are not of Christ—and thousands of people who think they are Christians because they "attend that church". The sad part is that they no longer belong to that first family—the family of God—because they have fallen away, being led by their own desires instead of the Spirit of God. They now belong to what we would call a knock-off version because it's no longer authentic with only Christ at the head.

A Christian's greatest enemy is deception! It comes at us subtly and through people and places we'd least expect it—inside the church! The devil first came to the Garden of Eden to deceive Eve and he succeeded. Why? Because she was deceived into thinking that she could serve God by doing her own thing. And while the devil continues to sow havoc in the world, his greatest battlefield and most rewarding encounter is the church. Discord is sown, itching ears listen, and weak or pretence Christians leave the fold to follow a wrong doctrine because it's so much easier than following the real one. In other words, they feel that they can serve God without parting from Satan's world.

If the church had kept its eyes on Christ and had never wavered at the first conflict that created divisions to satisfy its people, it would be strong today AND there would be only one church. This is why we're told to not fellowship with those who cause discord from the body of Christ; in fact, we're told to put them out of the church so that the faithful won't be tainted by the deception of the discord. It won't stop new doctrines from happening, but it will keep those who want only the gospel of Christ to be free of the temptation of deception.

141

Ronnie Dauber

> And have no fellowship with the unfruitful
> works of darkness, but rather reprove them.—
> Ephesians 5:11

The good news is, though, that Jesus is coming back as King over the whole earth, and He will establish His kingdom on earth and there will be ONLY ONE CHURCH and He alone will be the head. No divisions; no deceptions. One doctrine! But it will be too late to discover the truth then. We need to know that we are saved and walking according to His gospel now, while there is still time. And to do that we have to study the scriptures and know the truth so we will not be deceived into following deception and adding to the discord.

> And He is before all things, and by Him all
> things consist. 18And He is the head of the
> body, the church: who is the beginning, the
> firstborn from the dead; that in all things He
> might have the pre-eminence."—Colossians
> 1:17-18

Perils of Gossip

Most of us enjoy talking and sharing with our family and friends, and it's even normal for us to pour our heart out in anguish about a situation or person that has hurt and challenged us. We're told in James 5:16 to share with each other so that we can pray for each other, and where many of these issues remain private to the glory of God, many more become public ridicule and the targets of gossip.

Christians can fall into the perils of gossiping as easily as anyone of the world when they don't keep control over their tongue. Yet, it's often more than just a slip of the tongue that turns into gossip. Often, it's an intentional tactic, although perhaps not totally realized, that weak or so-called Christians use to build themselves up. What better way to make themselves look like a good Christian than to expose someone else's faults? They build up their own SELF-esteem to others to make themselves appear very (self) righteous before them because, after all, they would never do those terrible things!

There is this foolish idea within some of us that if we constantly expose the faults of others, we'll stand out as the better Christian; people will look at us and say, "Oh, how that Christian is so informed and wise and living as Christ. I wish I could be like them." The truth is that they are living the opposite to Christ! They are deceivers and if they are given the ability, they will draw others away from God.

Jesus told us repeatedly to "preach the gospel"—the good news! He told us to tell everyone that He is the Son of God, who came to earth as the Lamb of God to die on the cross and take away our sins, that God raised Him from the dead and that He now lives in Heaven as our Lord and Savior, and our King! He told us to spread this message of hope to everyone so they, too, could be born-again and become part of God's kingdom, and have an eternal home in Heaven with Jesus.

> And He said to them, 'Go into all the world and preach the gospel to every creature.'— Mark 16:15

Jesus told us to tell the people of the world that they need to repent of their sins and turn to Him for salvation. He told us to correct Christians when they need it so they can live a proper Christian life. Through the scriptures, we can show God's love and forgiveness and grace to them now so they can see the error of their way and turn to Christ for direction.

> All scripture is given by inspiration of God, and is profitable for doctrine, for reproof, for correction, for instruction in righteousness.— 2 Timothy 3:16

As well, God told us that if, when attempting to correct Christians individually in a private manner, they refuse to heed to our words, then we are to present them to the elders of the church so they can step in and hopefully bring the party or parties to repentance. And if that doesn't work, then we're told that these individuals are to be put out of the congregation and that we should separate ourselves from them.

> Moreover if thy brother shall trespass against thee, go and tell him his fault between thee and him alone: if he shall hear thee, thou hast gained thy brother. 16 But if he will not hear thee, then take with thee one or two more, that in the mouth of two or three witnesses every word may be established. 17 And if he shall neglect to hear them, tell it unto the church:

but if he neglect to hear the church, let him be
unto thee as an heathen man and a
publican.—Matthew 18:15-17

But nowhere in the scriptures does it say to
repeatedly gossip about them and present them to the world
as backsliders. Nowhere in the scriptures does it say to
constantly make conversations about them and pass the
gossip about them onto others. In fact, we're told just the
opposite. We're told in 1 Timothy 5:13 that we are not to
gossip! And we will be held accountable as Christians for all
those idle words that we do speak.

But I say unto you, 'That every idle word that
men shall speak, they shall give account
thereof in the day of judgment'.—Matthew
12:36

Sometimes we feel that we're doing the world a great
justice by constantly bringing to its attention the fallacies that
we find in someone or in specific "Christian" ministries. It's
true that both the Christian world and the unsaved world need
to know that there are false teachers and preachers out there,
and it's good to warn them when necessary. It's essential that
these "wolves" are exposed so that innocent people can
become aware of their antics and stop following their false
religion. But we have to be wise about when and under what
circumstances we discuss these faults because the world is
watching, and it's making its own opinion of the Christian
realm, be it real or just proclaiming Christians. When we
spend our time running down other Christians and their
ministries, it reaffirms to the world what they already
believe—that there is no unity in Christianity and that there is
more animosity amongst Christians than there is in the world.

We cannot let this motive overtake us so that we
make it our lifelong ministry to expose others instead of

preaching the gospel. Apostle Paul taught us to be like the Bereans—Acts 17:11—and to judge the doctrines and teachers by comparing what is being taught to the scriptures. But their false doctrines shouldn't become our prime objective. Jesus called us to be His disciples who share the truth about God, about His love and grace, and to preach the gospel of Jesus unto salvation. This brings glory to God; spreading rumors only gives glory to the devil.

> For there are many unruly and vain talkers and deceivers, specially they of the circumcision: 11 Whose mouths must be stopped, who subvert whole houses, teaching things which they ought not, for filthy lucre's sake.—Titus 1:10-11

Christians are fighting more now than ever before to keep the love of God and the salvation message of Christ alive, and the enemy is working just as hard to destroy the Christians' testimony. The world is watching and when it sees that our love and faithfulness to God prevails, it sees our hope and many are encouraged to accept Jesus!

But when Christians spend their time criticizing, judging and tearing each other down, the world watches and concludes that being a Christian is a joke. When the issues of the false preachers and prosperity teachers become the focal point of our existence to the world, it sees us as obsessed critics and it doesn't want anything to do with God or with Christians because it brands us all as being liars and two-faced extremists. And when we spend our time spreading rumors about false leaders instead of sharing the good news, we let the world see just another piece of itself instead of the love of God that they should see through us.

We need to choose today who we will serve. We need to stay focused on Jesus and show the world that He is a God of love and forgiveness because He came to earth and died on that cross to take our sins away. And we also must show the world that He is a God of justice and one day all sin will be judged by Him, and if sin is found in us, we will be judged instead of pardoned. We need to focus on Christ and train our tongue to glorify Him only.

> And He said unto them, 'Go ye into all the world, and preach the gospel to every creature'.—Mark 16:15-16

Ronnie Dauber

A Doctrine of Hate

Besides spreading rumors, there are so-called Christians who feel it's their given ministry to keep us up-to-date on the actions and lives of religious leaders and false teachers. They make it their daily quest to ridicule and mock those who, in their opinion, are less Godly than themselves. And unfortunately, while other so-called Christians have itching ears for this gossip, the world watches and concludes that the church is actually the root of much hatred. We're not drawing people closer to Jesus when we do this; we're pushing them away as we mock God with what appears to them to be a doctrine of hate!

Christians are all saved by the grace of God! Not a single one of us has earned it or deserve it. And when we study the scriptures we learn how to please God and what His commission is for us, and it's not to build a ministry on hatred.

> For all have sinned, and come short of the glory of God; 24 Being justified freely by his grace through the redemption that is in Christ Jesus.—Romans 3:23-24.

It's good that we are aware of false teachers and preachers and it's also right that we let others know not to follow them. Jesus warns us in Matthew 7:15, "Beware of false prophets, which come to you in sheep's clothing, but inwardly they are ravening wolves." But it's wrong to make it a daily quest to see what dirt we can find on them so we can constantly degrade and ridicule them on online public media sites. It seems that some Christians spend more time at this than they do at being a witness for Christ—and the world is watching. This is not what Jesus told us to do. He told us to beware of false teachers and to expose them when necessary, but our commission is to preach the gospel and get people saved.

> And He said unto them, 'Go ye into all the world, and preach the gospel to every creature'.—Mark 16:15

It's so obvious why the "new age religion" is overwhelming multitudes with its deceiving message! So many people who call themselves Christians are showing themselves to be hypocrites who preach one thing and then do quite another. This new age move sees the old-time religion as being the false gospel, and we have let that happen through our own actions. The new age religion says that Jesus died for everyone and so everyone is automatically saved. No need for repentance, no need to change your lifestyle. Jesus said, "It is finished" and to them, that means that all humanity has been redeemed.

And there are countless people who are going to stand before God at the Great White Throne and be told that they'll spend eternity in darkness because they were not saved. Some of these people might be our own loved ones and friends. They are being drawn in to the heresy of this new age religion because there is a bonding of love and respect between them that is clearly not being seen in many so-called Christians today.

And so Christians are being referred to as haters because of the way they purportedly treat others. And although this new religion is on the wrong path, the people are committed to each other, and they support each other and they don't condemn anyone. It will continue to grow and deceive thousands of people because there is a common unity among them that inspires others to want to be part of it. Everyone is equal, no one is wrong, and life is good.

And if these "Christians" aren't making public critical statements about various ministries, they're speaking badly about individuals. This type of gossip is destructive because as Christians, we are all on the narrow path heading toward God, but we are not all in the same place on the same path at the same time. So it's wrong for other Christians to look back at the new or immature ones and criticize them. What we need to do is love them and pray for them and encourage them toward Jesus.

> Let the word of Christ dwell in you richly in all wisdom; teaching and admonishing one another in psalms and hymns and spiritual songs, singing with grace in your hearts to the Lord.—Colossians 3:16

With the freedom of speech on the internet today, there are many so-called Christians writing on blog posts and social media sites and they mock others publically who they feel are heretics or who they say were never saved. These social religious critics only post when they're criticizing or making fun of others, and while they give the impression that they are helping the rest of us to stay clear of these people, we have to wonder if they're not just having fun at their cynical destruction of others. Regardless, their message is two-fold; it's showing Christians that we need to stay clear of people that we don't really know the truth about, and it's showing the world that they need to stay clear of us.

Our testimony may be the only witness of God that some people will ever see! And so we need to walk in the love of Jesus, be the "light" that He's told us to be, and preach His salvation message so they can find Him and repent and be saved from the wrath to come. We are the light in this dark world and we need to let it shine as lighthouses for others to see, not as daunting flash lights in the shadows for others to mock.

150

> Ye are the light of the world. A city that is set
> on an hill cannot be hid.—Matthew 5:14

Those who live to mock others don't realize the damage they're doing, not only by giving a bad testimony as a Christian, but also to themselves. Not one of us has the right to judge and condemn another person no matter what that other person is doing. They may be a false teacher or perhaps living a lifestyle that is not pleasing to God according to the scriptures, but that does not give any of us the right to judge them. Some of these Christians feel that they have that right. But warning us through scripture that they are heretics is one thing; judging them and saying who is going to hell is totally out of their jurisdiction and it's something they'll truly regret if they don't stop now!

The Book of Life has not been opened and when it is opened the only one who worthy to read from it is Jesus Christ. And until that book is opened, there is not one person on earth who can know whose name won't be in that book. God says that only He knows the heart of man, and so the very person that's being mocked could easily see that Jesus is real and repent at the last second. No Christian should attempt to raise him or herself up to the seat of Christ and judge others in this way. Look what happened to the devil when he tried to make himself equal with God!

Every saved person—Christian—is a part of God's family, and as members of this family we need to be careful that we don't criticize or condemn someone who has accepted Christ as their savior just because "we" don't think they did. And when we learn that a false preacher is ill or dying, we shouldn't joke about it or speak badly about it. This is a person who will spend eternity in hell if they die before they get saved. This is not an opportunity to gloat in our own (self) righteousness. Jesus said to pray for our enemies—Matthew 5:44. This is an opportunity to get on our knees and plead for their lives before Christ, and ask Him to send laborers to witness to them and pray with this person. We have all sinned against God, and just because we accepted Christ as our Savior years ago doesn't mean that God loves us more than the person who took their lifetime to find Him.

> Likewise, I say unto you, there is joy in the presence of the angels of God over one sinner that repenteth.—Luke 15:10

Our commission is to preach the gospel and get people saved. Let's be obedient, walk in God's love and grace, and with peace show God to the world.

> Let him know, that he which converteth the sinner from the error of his way shall save a soul from death, and shall hide a multitude of sins.—James 5:20

An Experience of Humility

Corrie ten Boom wrote a book called The Hiding Place and it's the true story of how she not only survived the brutal concentration camps of WW2, but how she saved the lives of countless persecuted Christians. In spite of her own devastating circumstances, she continued to be the light to the other women in the camps. Corrie and her family endured horrors and tortures that most of us could never fathom and yet, God was right there with her, working through her so that she could be a blessing to the other suffering people. Her story is truly an experience of humility.

Most of us will never go through what Corrie ten Boom did, and most of us will never know what it's like to truly suffer for Christ. We live in a modern world that surrounds us with material possessions and congenial friends so that life is somewhat easy and comfortable. We lean on the world for the answers to our daily issues, and when tougher trials come some of us complain that we have to suffer through something that our televangelist promised God would exempt us from—after all, we are Christians. Many of us have lost our ability to be humble before God because we are following leaders who teach false doctrines that appease our personal desires and rights and don't submit to the authority of Christ.

> For the time will come when they will not endure sound doctrine; but after their own lusts shall they heap to themselves teachers, having itching ears; 4 And they shall turn away their ears from the truth, and shall be turned unto fables.—2 Timothy 4:3-4

We can't be fence sitting Christians anymore! We need to either dive deep into the Bible and study it diligently to know God and what His direction is for our lives, or we need to dive deep into the Bible and study it diligently to know God and what His direction is for our lives. In other words, if we're going to say that we're a Christian, then we need to get serious and be one! We need to stop playing games and choose who we will serve while we can still choose.

> And if it seem evil unto you to serve the Lord, choose you this day whom ye will serve; whether the gods which your fathers served that were on the other side of the flood, or the gods of the Amorites, in whose land ye dwell: but as for me and my house, we will serve the Lord.—Joshua 24:15

We can all look around us and see that the world is falling apart. The devil is busy destroying this world along with the people who God created to live in it. And he's moving faster and harder now because his time is almost over and he knows it. Jesus is about to return! We need to stop following false doctrines and showy preachers and get back to the basics—back to the Bible!

Christianity is not about us! It's not about what we can get from God, but rather, it's about what God has already given to us. He gave His life as a ransom for our sins. He gave us freedom from sin, and freedom from the punishment of that sin. He pardoned us from the wrath that is about to come upon this world and He gave us an eternal home in Heaven. We are not people of the world: we are the redeemed of Christ!

And we need to stop raising ourselves up and expecting life to come to us on a silver platter because it's not going to happen during this lifetime. Trials and tribulations are going to come simply because we live in a world that's corrupt and dying. We know that we don't belong here and so we need to preach about the salvation of Christ and the world to come!

> These things I have spoken to you, that in Me you may have peace. In the world you will have tribulation; but be of good cheer, I have overcome the world.—John 16:33

What Jesus suffered on the cross should bring us all to our knees. We should all be humbled and amazed that God could and would do this for us. He left His throne in Heaven to come to earth and become one of us—a human! The Bible says in Psalm 8:5 and in Hebrews 2:7 that Jesus became a little lower than the angels. He was God and yet He walked among us! How humbling is that! Yet, many Christians don't fully understand what God did for them. When Adam and Eve sinned and brought a curse upon the whole of mankind, God could have just walked away and left us alone until we became an extinct species. And without God's intervention throughout the years, sin truly would have killed us.

But God loved the world that He'd made and it was His desire that His children live in this paradise that He created. God had a plan to remove the sin that cursed His children and to defeat the devil that had set out to destroy the earth. And when we accept that Christ took our sins, we denounce sin and we accept Christ as our Lord and Savior. And then the old man in us (the old, sinful nature) dies and we are filled with the Spirit of God. Truly a humbling experience!

> Knowing this, that our old man is crucified with Him, that the body of sin might be destroyed, that henceforth we should not serve sin.—Romans 6:6

We study the Bible and accept it as true because it IS true. And the more we study, the more God reveals His truth to us. The human mind can't understand any of it and that's why false preachers don't teach the truth and that's why followers who don't know the truth will be deceived. But when we search and study the scriptures to know the truth, the Holy Spirit teaches us.

Jesus said in Matthew 5:14 that we are the light of the world. The world lives in darkness because it doesn't know God. The wages of its sin is death—Romans 6:23, and so anyone or anything linked with sin is heading towards hell. There aren't different levels of sin that qualify for different levels of punishment. The sacrifice of Christ covered all sin. We either have sin in us or we don't. We either serve Satan or we serve God.

We can read about the laws that God gave to Moses in Exodus 20, and He did this so that the people would have a guideline to live by, and every person was responsible to follow those laws. And if any part of any one of these laws was broken even in the slightest way, then a sin was committed. God knew that this was an impossible task because of the devil's influence, and so He appointed Moses' brother, Aaron, to be the first priest to receive sacrifices of atonement on a holy altar to the Lord. God then instructed Moses to build the Ark of the Covenant where the two tablets that contained the Ten Commandments would stay and be forever in the presence of the people. These laws were absolute and can never change because God doesn't change. They are still in effect today and the consequences of breaking them remains the same.

> For the wages of sin is death; but the gift of God is eternal life through Jesus Christ our Lord.—Romans 6:23

The difference between then and now is grace! Jesus tells us in Matthew 5:17 that He didn't come to change the law, but to fulfill the law! He came as the Lamb of God—(John 1:29)—to be the ultimate and final sacrifice that would bring God's people back to Him. So now, anyone who accepts Jesus as their Savior is saved from their sin and lives in grace—forgiveness. We are still obligated to obey the law, but we are no longer ruled by the law. We obey it with a willing heart and when we do something wrong—and we all do—we are not condemned for the sin, but have been given the grace to ask God to forgive us without needing another sacrifice, and that's because Jesus was the sacrifice.

Many people don't understand why some Christians spend their lives preaching and singing and living for God. And they won't know until they truly give their lives to Christ. Only then can anyone know the love that God has for them and that because of this love He saved them from their sins. Truly, we are humbled by His grace!

> That if thou shalt confess with thy mouth the Lord Jesus, and shalt believe in thine heart that God hath raised Him from the dead, thou shalt be saved.—Romans 10:9

The Deception of MY Faith

Religious leaders of many different doctrines seem to be focussing on faith today more than ever before, as if it's our faith that makes us successful in our endeavors. We may win battles and gain victories because of our faith, but let's give glory to the One who deserves it. And that person isn't "me"! We are all people in a big, corrupt world who need a Savior to take our sins away so that we can live in grace. And this grace comes to us through faith; a faith that some of us so blatantly brag about to our own glory—as in it's <u>my</u> faith!

The Bible tells us in Hebrews 11:1 that "faith is the substance of things hoped for; the evidence of things not seen". And the Webster's dictionary says that faith is "a strong belief or trust in someone or something". So basically, faith is a confidence we have in something or someone to bring something to pass. Now, there are two powers that influence us—the mighty power of God Almighty, and the power of darkness that rules this world and does not want us to know God. But, there is great danger when our faith is not in the Lord because then our faith lies within our own abilities that are influenced by this world. And this is when we begin to believe that through our own faith we have the power to speak things into being—making it "my faith".

Many of the televangelists and famous mega church preachers focus on the issue of our own faith as if we have the power to control and expand our faith. They teach that if we can just get our faith up there, we can have whatever we desire; we can avoid tribulation and live our best life now. It's not about having faith in God; it's about having faith in ourselves to believe.

God given faith:

Our minds are so influenced by sin and corruption that we are totally incapable through our own reasoning to grasp who God is or what His purpose is. It's impossible for us on our own to accept God's existence or to even comprehend that He could love us at all, or that He lives in Heaven where He's prepared a place for us. And this is because the spirit in unbelievers is subject only to the ruler of this world, which is the devil. So there are times in life when God gives to each of us a measure of faith—a seed; just enough for us to realize who God is and that we need Him. It's just enough faith to bring us to the cross of salvation, to encourage us to repent and turn from the world and accept Jesus as our Lord and Savior.

This first measure or seed of faith is a gift from God. It's a special means of spiritual understanding that allows us to reach up to God and it is the ONLY means given whereby we can find Him. This gift comes at those times when unbelievers are with people who are preaching or teaching or just witnessing about God's love. And it can come at a time when an unbeliever is at his or her lowest point and looking for help—even help from God.

> For by grace are ye saved through faith; and
> that not of yourselves: it is the gift of God:—
> Ephesians 2:8

Like any earthly seed that we plant, water and care for, our faith seed also needs to be planted and nourished so it can grow into something magnificent to the glory of God. And we do this by studying the scriptures to know God, praying to Him to develop our relationship with God, and worshiping Him so we bask in the glory of God. Faith was never given to us so we could brag about it or feel lifted up because of it. It was never meant to be abused, mistreated or used as a means for selfish gain. Faith is the "substance" (Hebrews 11:1) that brings us to God; it's the confidence or trust that we have towards God that gets stronger as we study the Bible and seek God's face.

Faith is not a magic concept that forces the universe to heed to our commands, nor is it a confession that makes us better than anyone else. There are ungodly preachers who teach that there is power in our words; in essence, exalting ourselves and denying the Lord. They say that if we confess our faith over and over and speak it out to the heavens that we will get the riches we declare because the heavens will finally open up to us.

There are prosperity leaders who promise that you can have what you say if you just have faith in your own words and confess them often—(not faith in God to provide, but in your own words to bring it to pass). This faith has nothing to do with God and didn't come from God, but rather, is a tactic used to encourage followers to give money to their ministries under the false pretence that it's giving in faith. It won't do a thing for the person giving their hard-earned dollars, but it sure helps to make those preachers live a life of abundance and luxury. It's flaunted before their congregations as a witness of what God will give when people have the faith—and the followers don't figure it out that the leader's riches are really dependent upon them to keep giving.

They call it faith, but it's not the faith that is given by God so we can know Him; it's a self-proclaimed faith that comes from a selfish heart and supposedly executes results through the power of the words spoken. This faith is more accurately a chant that is repeated through the confession of desires. It's the foundation for the false teaching that lures people away from the God of Heaven and onto the god of this world, who is all about lies and deception. This faith is about denying the truth and promoting the new age religion that supports the mandate for the Law of Attraction, a new age philosophy that you can research online at: http://www.thelawofattraction.com. This is "my faith" and has nothing to do with faith in God.

When Jesus talks about having faith as in a grain of mustard seed, He's not talking about confessions or name-it and claim-it actions. Jesus is talking about having faith or trust in God alone. When our knowledge and our trust in God are both mature, we can believe Him to do anything we ask. Of course, this also means that we would be mature enough to ask for things according to His will and not out of our selfish desires.

> And Jesus said unto them, 'Because of your unbelief: for verily I say unto you, If ye have faith as a grain of mustard seed, ye shall say unto this mountain, Remove hence to yonder place; and it shall remove; and nothing shall be impossible unto you.'—Matthew 17:20

It's not "my faith" that brings me to God or that brings blessing from God to me, or that allows me to rise up out of a sick bed, or that saves another lost soul. God brings these things to pass through my faith in Him to do so, but my faith alone can never manifest anything. The faith I have is a trust in God and it gives me the confidence to know that He will do what He promises to do.

Faith is accepting and trusting that God is who the Bible says He is and that His words are true. When our hope and our desires are in the Lord, then we know we please Him. And we know that one day He will look at us and His eyes will reflect a love that tells us we have pleased Him because we nurtured the faith He gave us and through it we were able to know Him.

> But without faith it is impossible to please him: for he that cometh to God must believe that he is, and that he is a rewarder of them that diligently seek him.—Hebrews 11:6

Ronnie Dauber

The Epitome of Forgiving

One of the greatest challenges that many of us face is the ability to forgive someone for hurting us. We can seem to follow Jesus in everything else except for this one very difficult task. Yet, it's a task that is totally necessary to be a Christian. It's what being a Christian is about. Our sins were forgiven at the cross and we were taken from a life that would have ended up with judgment against us to a life of freedom that gives us a home with Jesus forever. The cross shows us the importance of forgiving.

There are basically three types of forgiveness that we need to apply to our lives—and each one is crucial in our walk with God.

<u>Divine Forgiveness:</u>

We learn in Romans 6:23 that the wages sin is death, and in Psalm 55:15 we see that this death is destined to eternity in hell. When we accept Jesus as our Lord and Savior, all the sins we've ever committed are forgiven and every time we sin after that we can come to Him and repent and He will forgive us again—and again. His sacrifice pardoned us from those sins and God will never again acknowledge them again.

> For God so loved the world that He gave His
> only begotten Son, that whosoever believeth
> in Him should not perish, but have everlasting
> life.—John 3:16

The sinful nature that we inherited from Adam—the one that separated us from God—is gone! In 2 Corinthians 5:17 it says, "Therefore if any man be in Christ, he is a new creature: old things are passed away; behold, all things are become new."

162

We read in Galatians 3:13 that Christ redeemed us from the curse of the law and that our old nature was removed—that spirit of the world controlled by the devil—and we were filled with God's Spirit. Nothing can separate us from God and anything we do wrong after we are saved (and we all do things wrong) is immediately forgiven when repent for it. This freedom is called "living in grace".

However, this grace does not give us permission to deliberately sin and just assume that we are forgiven. It's a grace that allows us to repent and be forgiven when we do slip as we grow in the Lord. We'll pray for God's strength to help us along the way and ask Him to help us not to sin. But don't be fooled; if we don't repent of these sins we will have to answer to Jesus for them the day we stand before Him.

> For we must all appear before the judgment seat of Christ; that every one may receive the things done in his body, according to that he hath done, whether it be good or bad.—2 Corinthians 5:10

Forgiveness Between Each Other

There are times in life when we offend people, whether deliberately or unintentionally, and God expects us to ask them to forgive us so we can keep peace with them. There are other times that people offend us and God also expects us to accept their apology to keep peace with them. God wants His children to be at peace with each other, otherwise we're not obeying God and we won't have peace with Him, either.

> And be ye kind one to another, tenderhearted, forgiving one another, even as God for Christ's sake hath forgiven you.—Ephesians 4:32

Unfortunately, sometimes we won't have the ability to speak personally with someone who has offended us or who we have offended, but we can forgive them in our heart and not harbor bad feelings toward them. And then if the opportunity allows, we can speak to them in person.

There may be other times when our apology might not be accepted, but if we mean it then we'll have peace within ourselves and our heart and our conscience would be free even if they choose to hold onto their bad feelings towards us. We would have obeyed God and there would be peace between us and God, and that's what counts.

When the offense is great and we can't forgive someone on our own merits, then we ask God to give us a forgiving heart. Through the strength of the Holy Spirit we'll be able to forgive them and forget the hostility and the anger that we've carried towards them. We need to get rid of these bad feelings so the devil doesn't have any ground to work on.

> Create in me a clean heart, O God; and renew
> a right spirit within me.—Psalm 51:10

Then there will be those who habitually offend us and apologize without any genuine remorse or care—and this can be very frustrating. This bothered Apostle Peter, too, and so he asked Jesus how many times we have to forgive someone who does this.

> Then came Peter to him, and said, 'Lord, how
> oft shall my brother sin against me, and I
> forgive him? till seven times?' 22 Jesus saith
> unto him, 'I say not unto thee, Until seven
> times: but, Until seventy times seven'.—
> Matthew 18:21-22

According to Strong's Greek Concordance: 1441, the words "seventy times seven" are translated from the Greek words, "ἑβδομηκοντάκις ἑπτά", which mean countless times. The word "seven" is translated from the Greek word "teléo", which means "complete or finished"—Strong's Exhaustive Concordance: 5055.

So in essence, Jesus said we should forgive countless times—until it is finished—until it's not necessary to forgive anymore. And if someone won't accept our apology or won't forgive us, then they stand accountable to God; and we don't have to like them, but we will have peace.

> But if ye forgive not men their trespasses, neither will your Father forgive your trespasses.—Matthew 6:15

Self Forgiveness

Sometimes the most difficult person to forgive is our self. Perhaps we had an abortion, or maybe we had too much to drink and caused a car accident that killed or permanently injured someone, or perhaps we were unkind to someone and they died before we could make it right. Whatever the issue is, our thoughts are tormented as the unforgiving scene plays over and over in the cobwebs of our mind.

We live in constant agony over it and we inflict our own subconscious punishment for what we did because we will not—we cannot—forgive ourselves. But God can help us when we ask Him. We need to come to Him and ask Him to help us accept what happened and to help us to forgive ourselves so we can put it all behind us. Only God can give us the peace that we need to deal with this type of hurt and pain. And if it seems that God is taking a long time to help us, we have to realize that He is there the second we ask and that we are just taking a long time to let go.

> Come unto me, all ye that labour and are
> heavy laden, and I will give you rest.—
> Matthew 11:28

There's power in forgiveness!

Christ forgave us with His life on the cross and so we accept His grace and forgive others. We don't judge them and we don't have to like them, but we forgive them because Christ forgave us.

> Then said Jesus, 'Father, forgive them; for
> they know not what they do.'—Luke 23:34

Inner Battles that Destroy

We all have our own personal battles to fight. They come at us from different angles and with various degrees of force, but each one is a challenge and brings on some measure of stress. Many of us go though financial struggles, health issues, relationship problems, the death of a loved one or job stresses at some point in our life. Yet, as difficult as they are, it's the hidden battles behind these main situations that can cause the most damage. These are battles that we fight within our own being and are between our spirit and our flesh. It's a personal battlefield that's between what we want and what we know God wants for us. These are the inner battles that can destroy us the most!

Sometimes we'll work at something for ages and struggle to make it happen, yet we never succeed. We remain stubborn and determined to do it because we want it, and so we repeat our efforts over and over until the task becomes an obsession that grows with each passing day. Without realizing it, we have chosen to serve ourselves rather than God. We no longer function to please God, but to fulfill our own desires and lusts. And these desires slowly become our god.

> But every man is tempted, when he is drawn away of his own lust, and enticed.—James 1:14

We can know what God wants for us in our life when we study the Bible and spend time in prayer and worship with the Lord. This special time allows God's Holy Spirit who lives in us to minister to us, to teach us and reveal God's truth to us. If something is wrong for us, we'll get that bad feeling—our conscience, which is really God's Spirit guiding our inner thoughts, and it will tell us, "Don't do it". And we'll know that it's His will because we know the scriptures that verify the truth. And when something is right for us, we'll get an encouraging feeling; an inspiration to pursue the thing we're seeking. But when we don't know if it's from God or not, we should not react until we have searched the scriptures and spent time in prayer to get God's guidance on the issue.

> But God hath revealed them unto us by his
> Spirit: for the Spirit searcheth all things, yea,
> the deep things of God.—1 Corinthians 2:10

The danger comes when we want something because we want it—but it doesn't happen. This is when we get aggressive towards it and obsessed with it. But sometimes it doesn't happen because it's not what God wants for us, either at this time or perhaps ever. And sometimes deep down in we know that, but we want it anyway. We feel that we work hard and deserve this break, and what harm can it do? And while God does want us to prosper, He also wants us to stay within His will because this is what is best for us and He knows what the outcome of our desire will bring to our lives.

> Beloved, I wish above all things that thou
> mayest prosper and be in health, even as thy
> soul prospereth..—3 John 1:2

God knows everything and sees everything, and He is all wisdom and knowledge. We are limited in what we see and in what we know, and we cannot foresee the future. Sometimes the things we want will bring us hardship in the end or even worse, separation from God. Our human minds can't always know the outcome of our choices—and often we're too stubborn to want to know—but God knows. So we need to follow Him and let Him guide us; otherwise, we will one day face the consequences for our own actions and it may be worse than we ever imagined.

When we let our desires take over our thoughts and our hopes, we can miss God's will for our life and that is a very dangerous place to be. We never want to be outside of His will because that is where evil lurks; that is where we lose sight of God and get lured into the devil's clutches. He is the enemy out there who wants to steal our joy, kill our relationship with God and destroy us—(John 10:10). And we are susceptible to his attacks when we take our eyes off of God, step aside from His will, and follow our own desires.

> Be sober, be vigilant; because your adversary
> the devil, as a roaring lion, walketh about,
> seeking whom he may devour.—1 Peter 5:8

God wants to bless us and He WILL bless us with the things that He knows are good for us. But if we give all of our attention to accomplish something or to get something on our own merits, then we are no longer looking to God for the blessings, but to ourselves. And when we serve ourselves, we have a fool for a master.

> No man can serve two masters: for either he
> will hate the one, and love the other; or else
> he will hold to the one, and despise the other.
> Ye cannot serve God and mammon.—
> Matthew 6:24

When our heart wants to follow God and our mind wants to follow the things of this world, we have a mighty battle going on inside that needs to be addressed. We need to realize that this thing we're trying to do isn't working because God doesn't want it for us. If we can grasp that and then come to God in prayer and repent and give the whole situation to Him—and then TRUST HIM to make it all right—we will win that battle and any injuries we incurred in the fight will be healed. If we won't surrender to God and we continue to fight for what we want, we will eventually lose because we cannot fight against the god of this world within our own merits. And a battle won by our enemy is dangerous for us.

> For we wrestle not against flesh and blood, but against principalities, against powers, against the rulers of the darkness of this world, against spiritual wickedness in high places.—Ephesians 6:12

When we fight against God's will, we are acting in disobedience because God says in Matthew 6:10 that His will is to be done on earth as it is in Heaven. And we know that when Jesus comes back to rule over all of the earth that His will, in fact, *will* be done. But for now, we serve God with a committed heart and we strive to fulfill His commission, and that is to preach the gospel and show the love of God to others. When we do this, we show the world what God's will is for them now and throughout eternity.

God loves us and He wants to bless us, and we need to study the scriptures and develop a relationship with the Lord so that we can know what His will is for us and when our thoughts drift outside of His will. Then we will be prepared for the enemy when he attacks us and our thoughts wonder off with questions about different issues or with lusts of the flesh. We grow in the Lord and stand for what He wants and the devil will leave because he'll know that God is ruling in this area of our life. He may return, but in the same way, we can make him leave.

> Submit yourselves therefore to God. Resist the devil, and he will flee from you.—James 4:7

It's not always the challenges that come at us from the outside world that will do us the most harm. Sometimes it's the fight that comes when we put our will over the will of God; in other words, when we fight God. So the sooner we learn to follow Him instead of telling Him to let us lead, the sooner those inner battles will be over and the sooner we will be where God wants us to be—and that is not on the battleground with the enemy, but in God's will where He can protect us.

> And be not conformed to this world: but be ye transformed by the renewing of your mind, that ye may prove what is that good, and acceptable, and perfect, will of God.— Romans 12:2

A Mirror of Deceit

In today's world we have a whole array of false Christian doctrines spreading in epic proportions across the globe under the guise of Universal, Inclusion and Prosperity, to name a few. Through mega churches, smaller ministries and word-of-mouth, the true gospel of Christ is being diluted, modified and changed to suit the lusts of the flesh. Some believe that the Christian life is easy and comes with abundant prosperity and perfect health, and anything that gets in the way is from the devil and to be rebuked. Others feel that they all serve one god regardless of what they call him and regardless of what they believe. And still others feel that every human ever born is saved and going to Heaven and that hell is fabrication of "Christianity" that reveals a brutal god. Sadly, the devil has fooled many with theses lie as the followers stare blindly into a mirror of deceit.

> But though we, or an angel from heaven, preach any other gospel unto you than that which we have preached unto you, let him be accursed.—Galatians 1:8

Christianity is not about self indulgence and prosperity; this is a heresy that puts millions of lives at risk! These lies belong to the devil and he spreads them around so people will honor him instead of God. And people are soaking them up because they don't read the Bible, they don't know God and they have never come to the Lord in repentance and asked Him to come into their lives. Instead, they think that they can just come to God and demand whatever they want from Him because they are entitled to it all—after all, if God said it then we have to right to claim it. And as they rest their eyes onto the deceivers who are preaching, greed takes over their own minds and they strive to become as wealthy as their lying leaders.

> Ye are of your father the devil, and the lusts
> of your father ye will do. He was a murderer
> from the beginning, and abode not in the
> truth, because there is no truth in him. When
> he speaketh a lie, he speaketh of his own: for
> he is a liar, and the father of it.—John 8:44

The Bible is NOT a manual that we dissect so we can know how to be all we can be according to our own desires and lusts. It was given to us so we could know God and know how to live life according to HIS will. God is NOT our puppet, nor is He our servant. The Bible is NOT our personal book of formulas that we memorize to get what we can from God. Honoring "me" is not the focal point of the scriptures and any religion that says it's so is a lie! Jesus is the focal point of the entire Bible.

Christians need to study the Bible and learn about God. They need to get their priorities in order and realize that Jesus is not only the Savior for those who come to Him in repentance, but He is also the Judge over those who don't. He is the creator of the universe and of everything that exists on our planet. John 1:3 says, "All things were made through Him, and without Him nothing was made that was made." People are under *His* authority. He is God; He is our Father and we are His children, not His equal. Children honor their father; the father is not a slave to their demands!

> For as the heavens are higher than the earth,
> so are My ways higher than your ways, and
> My thoughts than your thoughts.—Isaiah 55:9

God is omnipresent—He is everywhere all the time and no person on earth has this power regardless of who they think they are.

> The eyes of the Lord are in every place, beholding the evil and the good.—Proverbs 15:3

God is omnipotent—He is all-powerful and nothing is impossible to Him. No person on earth has this much control over anyone or anything, but through deception they will lure in their victims and they will believe the lie that says God has made us all to be equal with Him.

> Not that we are sufficient of ourselves to think anything as of ourselves; but our sufficiency is of God.—2 Corinthians 3:5

God is omniscient—God knows everything. People can only attain a microscopic fraction of God's knowledge until we are with Him in eternity. We can't hide from Him, can't keep secrets from Him, and can't even have private thoughts apart from Him. He sees and knows everything. And He also knows the intent of our heart when we speak and when we move.

> Neither is there any creature that is not manifest in His sight: but all things are naked and opened unto the eyes of Him with whom we have to do.—Hebrews 4:13

Earth is not our home; it is not our eternal retirement resort; and it is not the place where we live in abundance outside of God. But it is the place where man has been tricked into believing that he is the head of his own life. In the same way that Satan deceived Eve into believing that she would know everything God knows and be entitled to everything God has, he is still deceiving people today. And many so-called "Christians" believe the lie that says they don't need to repent and that material wealth is good and that every lifestyle is acceptable to God. And the devil is able to give those that follow him a false peace so they'll think that they are all saved.

> For where your treasure is, there will your heart be also.—Matthew 6:21

Jesus tells us that the Christian life will be hard, that we will be persecuted and that our lives will suffer constant abuse from the world because of Him. The world hates Christians because it is ruled by the devil who hates God, and if we are saved and live according to God's laws then we will be mocked and we will be hated just like Jesus was hated—not admired and accepted like a celebrity.

> And ye shall be hated of all men for my name's sake: but he that endureth to the end shall be saved.—Matthew 10:22

We're told in 3 John 1:2 that God wants us to prosper and be in health "even as our soul prospers". Unfortunately, heretic doctrines teach that this means God wants us to be rich and abundant in material possessions. But "prosperity" isn't just about material riches; it also means "affluence, success, a good reputation". God wants us to be successful in all that HE has set out for us to do—and that means spreading the message of the gospel so others can be saved; and it means loving others and helping them and treating them with the same love that Christ has for us. When we seek God only for material wealth, it separates us from Him and that wealth becomes our god.

> For the love of money is the root of all evil: which while some coveted after, they have erred from the faith, and pierced themselves through with many sorrows.—Timothy 6:10

We need to protect ourselves and not let anything this world has to offer separate us from the love of God. He does not pull away from us; we pull away from Him when our own lusts and desires take priority over His will. We need to flee from any person or any "ministry" that preaches any gospel other than the gospel of Jesus Christ.

> I marvel that ye are so soon removed from him that called you into the grace of Christ unto another gospel: 7 Which is not another; but there be some that trouble you, and would pervert the gospel of Christ. 8 But though we, or an angel from heaven, preach any other gospel unto you than that which we have preached unto you, let him be accursed. 9 As we said before, so say I now again, if any man preach any other gospel unto you than that ye have received, let him be accursed.— Galatians 1:6-9

God does answer our prayers and He meets our needs and even gives us the desires of our heart when we love Him and respect Him as our God and Heavenly Father. But we need to be responsible and seek after Him and not settle for a false image in the mirror of deceit.

> Blessed is the man that endureth temptation: for when he is tried, he shall receive the crown of life, which the Lord hath promised to them that love him.—James 1:12

The Object of the Cross

As Christians, we all know that Jesus is the Messiah who came to take away the sins of the world. Salvation is not just a general observation or an eternal assumption for everyone, but rather, it's a personal commitment that never ends. YOU are the reason He came—and YOU were the object of the cross!

Jesus came from the holiness of Heaven to live as a man on earth. He is the spoken word of God who came to live in a body for our sake. John 1:14 says, " And the Word was made flesh, and dwelt among us, (and we beheld his glory, the glory as of the only begotten of the Father,) full of grace and truth." This was a deliberate action of Jesus as He knew that He was to be the Lamb of God who would be sacrificed for our sins so that all of our sins would be pardoned and we would free of the curse of the law. John 1:29 says, "Behold the Lamb of God, which taketh away the sin of the world." He did this because He loves us. He was willing to become the ultimate sacrifice for us so that we could be saved from the wrath and judgment of God that will soon come upon this earth.

> For God so loved the world that He gave His
> only begotten Son, that whosoever believeth
> in Him should not perish, but have everlasting
> life.—John 3:16

God loves every person who was ever born, BUT not every person will accept His love and His salvation for them. Only those who accept it, believe it, repent from their old life and serve Him will be saved. Some false doctrines today teach that everyone is automatically saved because it says, "For God so loved the world"—John 3:16, and "It is finished"—John 19:30. But they don't want to change their lifestyle or make a commitment, so they don't obey what Jesus said and that is to repent and be born again.

> There was a man of the Pharisees, named Nicodemus, a ruler of the Jews: 2 The same came to Jesus by night, and said unto him, Rabbi, we know that thou art a teacher come from God: for no man can do these miracles that thou doest, except God be with him. 3 Jesus answered and said unto him, Verily, verily, I say unto thee, Except a man be born again, he cannot see the kingdom of God. 4 Nicodemus saith unto him, How can a man be born when he is old? can he enter the second time into his mother's womb, and be born? 5 Jesus answered, Verily, verily, I say unto thee, Except a man be born of water and of the Spirit, he cannot enter into the kingdom of God. 6 That which is born of the flesh is flesh; and that which is born of the Spirit is spirit.—John 3:1-6

When the disciples were preaching the gospel of Christ, they taught the people that to be born again they needed to repent of their sins and then turn away from that old lifestyle and follow Jesus. Salvation was not an assumption! It was (and still is) an actual heart-felt change that they had to make.

> Then Peter said unto them, 'Repent, and be baptized every one of you in the name of Jesus Christ for the remission of sins, and ye shall receive the gift of the Holy Ghost'.—Acts 2:38

> Therefore if any man be in Christ, he is a new creature: old things are passed away; behold,

all things are become new.—2 Corinthians
5:17

People can identify with Jesus as the one in the Bible who died on the cross, but this is not an automatic membership into Heaven. Even the devil knows who Jesus is, but he's been sentenced to hell already—James 2:19. We need to realize that we are sinners in need of a savior, and then we need to accept that God Himself provided a means for us to be forgiven of those sins. And He provided this for every single person ever born because He loves every single person ever born. But, it requires a personal acceptance from the heart from each individual who has found Him; not just acknowledgment in the mind followed by a notion that says everything is okay.

Many people cannot understand or appreciate the depth of God's love for us. He actually loves all people, but unfortunately, many people don't want His love. They mock Jesus, persecute Christians and enjoy living in the sinful world. They like who they are and they don't care about God. Yet, God continues to love them and is the force behind Christians getting out there and preaching to them so they'll get saved. We read in John 3:15 that God doesn't want a single person to die lost.

Some people think that God hates the people of the world and is taking pleasure in sending them to hell. But the truth is that He hates the sin in the world and the lifestyle that is killing His children. He hates sin and sin will be judged by the law one day and anyone found with sin in them will be judged, but He doesn't want anyone going to hell. We could better understand this if we saw it from the viewpoint of an earthly parent.

Suppose you had two children and both challenged your parenting skills as they were growing up. One child got into messes, but never failed to show their love to you and ask for your forgiveness, and they always respected you and honored you. They weren't perfect, but they loved you and you knew it. The other child, however, fell into the lifestyle of a bad crowd and was doing things that were not only wrong, but were dangerous for their own soul. You warned them and pleaded with them to change because if they continued on, you knew that they just may go too far and not be able to turn back. But they ignored you, cursed your ideals and continued anyway. And then one day, they committed a hideous crime and had to stand before a judge.

As a parent, your heart would ache more than you could ever imagine because you know that this child who you love so much will now forever be separated from you. You know that the judge will sentence your child for the crime that will send them to a dark prison for the rest of his or her life and they risk the death penalty. As loving parents, you would be totally sick from the agony of this ordeal.

This is how God sees things, too! He loves us all so much, but not every child will listen to Him or obey Him, and when people leave this earth they won't automatically go to Heaven. They first have to stand before the greatest judge of all—Jesus—who will weigh their actions against the law. It's the law, God's laws given to Moses in Exodus 20 that will judge them, and it's Christ who will sentence them because they didn't accept His pardon for their sins. And they now stand alone in front of Him wearing all their sins and nothing to save them.

God loves us all with so much passion that He constantly arranges situations for the unsaved people to accept Him, but the time is growing short and the devil is working hard to keep the people of the world from finding Him. And even though God loves us all, only those who "—

believeth in Him" will not perish on the day of judgment, "but will have everlasting life"—John 3:16.

There's still time to pray for the lost people of this world and to do all we can do to reveal Jesus to them. We need to work together and fight the good fight of faith and get the message of the gospel out there. People's lives literally depend on it, and eternity is a long time to spend in a dark, evil place separated from God. We are the object of the cross and we need to share God's truth with others so they can know it, too.

> Enter ye in at the strait gate: for wide is the gate, and broad is the way, that leadeth to destruction, and many there be which go in thereat: 14 Because strait is the gate, and narrow is the way, which leadeth unto life, and few there be that find it.—Matthew 7:13-14

The Sting of Death

No matter how careful we live our life or what diet regime we adapt to stay healthy we will all still die sometime. And far too many people have no idea where they're going when they die. Many assume they'll go to Heaven; some don't care; and others live in constant fear of the sting of death!

Death is nothing to fear—nor is it something to take lightly. Our body will die, but our soul will live on forever and it's crucial that we know where we're going when we leave our body. There are only two destinations: Heaven or hell. And it's OUR choice as to which one we will go to.

Contrary to the lies of the new age church and the inclusion doctrine, not everyone will go to Heaven. God loved the world—His creation—so much that He sent Jesus to come to earth to save us all—John 3:16-17—but let's not be so callous that we accept His sacrifice as a mere assumption. Salvation was given to everyone, but not everyone will accept it.

Some blatantly refuse to accept it and prefer to live "their best life now". Others just assume they're saved because the false doctrine they follow says they are, and it's this deception that will shock many when they face Jesus on Judgment Day.

> Not everyone that saith unto me, 'Lord, Lord', shall enter into the kingdom of heaven; but he that doeth the will of my Father which is in heaven. 22 Many will say to me in that day, Lord, Lord, have we not prophesied in thy name? and in thy name have cast out devils? and in thy name done many wonderful works? 23 And then will I profess unto them, I never

knew you: depart from me, ye that work iniquity.—Matthew 7:21-23

When Jesus died on the cross and spoke His last words, "It is finished", many lazy and uncommitted, so-called believers want that to mean that He died for everyone and now we're all saved from sin. These foolish people think that they will go to Heaven when they die and they'll continue to live their lives apart from God now. But this is NOT what Jesus meant when He spoke these words.

Jesus was saying that the plan of salvation, which God had put forward from the beginning of time, was now completed. Jesus, the Son of God, became the "Lamb of God" and was crucified on the cross for our sins. And in His last breath in His human body, Jesus declared that His mission was finished. He had provided a means whereby our sins could be pardoned.

It is wrong to assume that His words, "It is finished", are an automatic membership into Heaven for every person who ever lived. The Bible clearly says that not everyone who says, "Lord, Lord" will get into Heaven—Matthew 7:21. It is a lie to say that salvation is an automatic grace for everyone whether they believe in God or not. Yet, this false doctrine is keeping multitudes from receiving their salvation because they just assume that they're going to Heaven when they die.

When we read the New Testament, we learn clearly that the onus of salvation is on us. Apostle Paul says in Philippians 2:12 that we need to "work out your own salvation with fear and trembling". In other words, it's our responsibility to find it and receive it. It's our responsibility to know that we are sinners in need of a Savior and it's our responsibility to act on it. If we are serious about serving God, He will arrange for us to know the truth, but we need to act on it.

1: We need to first accept God as being the creator, lord, and king of this world.

> But without faith it is impossible to please Him: for he that cometh to God must believe that He is, and that He is a rewarder of them that diligently seek Him.—Hebrews 11:6

2: We must accept that Jesus is the Son of God who left Heaven to come to earth, that He was born as a man, that He died on the cross for our sins, that He was buried, and that He was raised on the third day, and now sits on His throne on the right side of God.

> That if thou shalt confess with thy mouth the Lord Jesus, and shalt believe in thine heart that God hath raised him from the dead, thou shalt be saved. 10 For with the heart man believeth unto righteousness; and with the mouth confession is made unto salvation.—Romans 10:9-10

3: We need to repent of our sins. We all belonged to this world at one time, but once we find Jesus we no longer want to serve the god of this world. And so we turn to the Lord, ask Him to forgive us and accept His pardon for us (in other words, we repent of our sins and give them to Christ) and then we can be free of them.

> From that time Jesus began to preach, and to say, 'Repent: for the kingdom of heaven is at hand'.—Matthew 4:17

> And the times of this ignorance God winked at; but now commandeth all men everywhere to repent.—Acts 17:30

4: We need to turn away from our sinful lifestyle and follow Jesus. This means leaving an adulterous relationship or a dishonest job; it means being honest and upright in all things; and it means that the sinful world we once enjoyed is now not an option or a desire. We turn away from it because the Spirit in us no longer belongs to this world, but to God.

> Then Peter said unto them, 'Repent, and be baptized every one of you in the name of Jesus Christ for the remission of sins, and ye shall receive the gift of the Holy Ghost'.— Acts 2:38

5: Then we are born again! Our sins are washed away and we are filled with God's Holy Spirit. Now we are able to study the Bible under His guidance and learn all truth. We have a direct line to God our Father through His Spirit in us.

> Jesus answered and said unto him, 'Verily, verily, I say unto thee, Except a man be born again, he cannot see the kingdom of God'.— John 3:3

It is absolutely crucial that we don't think or assume we are saved; it's absolutely imperative that we KNOW we are saved! And then we'll have peace because we'll know that when our time in this life is over, Jesus will send His angels to come and get us and take us home to Heaven to be with Him forever. No sting in death. Just perfect peace!

> In my Father's house are many mansions: if it were not so, I would have told you. I go to prepare a place for you. And if I go and prepare a place for you, I will come again, and receive you unto myself; that where I am, there ye may be also.—John 14:2-3

Ronnie Dauber

Oh, the Tragedy of the Missing Parachute

So often in life people take things for granted. Some assume that their way is the right way and they aren't willing to change or listen to suggestions for a better answer, even though their way isn't really working for them. Others know that they should act on certain issues now, but they either render a callous attitude and put it off until later, or do nothing and just assume that things will work out in the end. Unfortunately, this attitude can lead to the same detriment as the lonely pilot. He never bothered to check his safety equipment and when his engine failed he assumed that there was backup equipment, but was devastated when he faced the tragedy of the missing parachute.

The danger of putting things off until tomorrow is that not one of us is guaranteed a tomorrow. The Bible says in Psalm 118:24 that "this is the day the Lord has made". And in Matthew 6:34 we're told not to worry about tomorrow. In Lamentations 3:22-23 we read that God's mercies are new every morning. So today is only the day that we have because tomorrow is not here yet.

Christians who know and love the Lord are prepared to face God when they leave this world. They study the Bible and do God's will as best they can, and they know that even though there will be tribulation between now and then, God will bring them through it all and will welcome them Home to Heaven when this life is over, just as He promised. But many people don't bother to study the Bible to know God or His will and go through life and just "assume" that Heaven is their eternal home. They aren't prepared to go there and have no confirmation that they will go there. They don't repent and submit their lives over to Jesus; they just assume that their life is worthy of Heaven. But no one gets to Heaven through the doorway of assumption; everyone must go through Jesus

186

who said, "I am the door: by me if any man enter in, he shall be saved".—John 10:9

There are two main reasons why people don't repent for their sins in preparation for death.

One is that they assume we're all saved and headed for Heaven because Jesus died on the cross for everyone. They proclaim to be "Christians", but they don't believe that they need to repent for their sins; they just need to acknowledge that Jesus died on the cross. And they assume that they'll go to Heaven when they die because after all, God IS love and a loving God surely doesn't send people to hell—if there even really is a hell. They take Jesus' words, "It is finished", to mean that now every single person is automatically forgiven for their sins and will go to Heaven when they die. But that's not what this means! Jesus was saying that the plan God had initiated to redeem His children was now complete; that Jesus had become the ultimate "Lamb of God" who would take away the sins of the world; and that no other sacrifice was necessary. The redemption plan was finished.

It's a false doctrine that says there is no need for repentance, and that regardless of whether we believe in God or not, upon death we will all stand in the presence of God, realize and acknowledge who He is, and be welcomed into Heaven. This is a very foolish and "anti-Christ" attitude because we're told in James 2:19 that even "the devil believes and trembles", but he sure isn't going to Heaven. Every one of us is lost—doomed for judgment and punishment for our sins—and will stand before Christ to be judged unless we repent and accept Christ as our Savior, our Redeemer. Those who don't have the Spirit of God in them when they leave this world will stand before Christ to be judged by the law for all the sin that is in them. And many will be shocked!

And then will I profess unto them, I never knew you: depart from me, ye that work iniquity.—Matthew 7:23

Then shall he say also unto them on the left hand, Depart from me, ye cursed, into everlasting fire, prepared for the devil and his angels.—Matthew 25:41

Jesus said, "It is finished" because He had fulfilled the promise of God that was prophesied by the prophets throughout the Old Testament. There was nothing more to do as God had now provided the way for all of mankind to be saved from the punishment for their sins. He had made a pardon for them IF they would accept it. It was finished!

For God so loved the world, that He gave His only begotten Son, that whosoever believeth in Him should not perish, but have everlasting life. 17 For God sent not His Son into the world to condemn the world; but that the world through Him might be saved.—John 3:16-17

The second excuse is that so-called Christians don't take God or Heaven seriously. They would rather live now and worry about Heaven later. And this is just like the foolish pilot who didn't have a parachute. He didn't worry about it and assumed that if he ever needed one it would be there, so why bother looking for it now? The problem is that no one knows what the future holds, when it will be their turn to die, or even if they'll have time to think about a "parachute" when facing an unexpected death.

People look at Heaven as a place where they'll live after death, but what they don't realize is that "life" really begins here on earth and continues throughout eternity; it doesn't begin at eternity. For the Christian, life begins when we give our heart to Jesus. Earth is the battleground where we fight to share the gospel and love of God with others, and Heaven is at the end of the narrow path that we are traveling on, where we will live with our Lord in peace and joy forever. For those who don't come to Jesus and repent, they live on the broad path and are following it to their destruction into an eternity where they will forever be separated from Jehovah God, but always be in the presence of the god they served on earth; the devil.

> Enter ye in at the strait gate: for wide is the gate, and broad is the way, that leads to destruction, and many there be which go in there at: Because strait is the gate, and narrow is the way, which leads unto life, and few there be that find it.—Matthew 7:13-14

Jesus tells a story about a rich fool who refused to share his wealth with the poor and who even made sure that they didn't eat his crumbs. He was pleased with himself and loved his riches, and assumed that one day he would make it right with God, but for now he wanted to bask in his wealth. However, he died that night and never got that one last chance to repent and come to Christ. His assumption didn't get him into Heaven, but rather, it left him devastated as he really thought that God would have mercy on him and let him in. We're told that he looked up from the burning flames of hell and asked Abraham to allow Lazarus, the poor beggar who he'd denied the crumbs, to give him some water. But Abraham told him:

> Remember that thou in thy lifetime received thy good things, and likewise Lazarus evil things: but now he is comforted, and thou art tormented.—Luke 16:19-25

We really do reap what we sow. And if we want to ensure that Heaven is our eternal home, then we need to sow our faith in Christ now! And that means not assuming that we are going there because Jesus died on the cross, but knowing that we are going there because we have come to Jesus, repented for our sins and accepted His salvation. And it's something we do NOW. We don't put it off.

> Then Peter said unto them, 'Repent, and be baptized every one of you in the name of Jesus Christ for the remission of sins, and ye shall receive the gift of the Holy Ghost'.— Acts 2:38

Yes, Jesus died for everyone, but only those who have repented and been cleansed by His blood and reborn in His Spirit will follow Him into Heaven. Jesus becomes our "parachute" in life, the One who saves us from sure death. But those who just assume they are saved will be like the pilot who faced the tragedy of a "missing parachute". Don't put it off; don't assume anything. Go to Jesus now and repent while there's still time.

> Jesus answered and said unto him, 'Verily, verily, I say unto thee, Except a man be born again, he cannot see the kingdom of God'.— John 3:3

Repentance or Shortcut

Our world is quickly racing towards convenience and short cuts in almost every facet of life. The things that used to require time and effort can now be accomplished online in seconds—things such as banking, paying bills, shopping, ordering a meal and even securing lucrative employment. These conveniences require little effort and almost no thought as we take for granted what technology has given us—short cuts! We just click a button and we have instant success. However, when we're looking for salvation, there are no shortcuts.

Many people want to become Christians because they want to go to Heaven when they leave earth, and they want to enjoy the blessings of God while they're here. But they don't want to change who they are or put any effort into being a Christian. They look for the shortest and easiest way to become a Christian that requires the least amount of effort to gain instant results. And the world has offered a shortcut under the guise of Christianity that millions of people are falling prey to.

There is a false doctrine spreading like fire across the globe—the Inclusion doctrine— and it teaches that Jesus died and saved all of mankind at the cross, regardless of whether you accept it now or not. It proclaims that when each of us gets to Heaven, we'll be judged on how well we loved our neighbour and it uses what Jesus said in Luke 10:27 as their basis for their Christianity, and that is that we are to love our neighbor as we love ourselves.

The Inclusion doctrine twists the scripture at John 3:16 to mean that every person ever born is automatically included in this salvation. It teaches that hell is the destination for the devil and his angels only, and that no loving God would send a person there; therefore, no human is going to be there. It teaches that if someone doesn't acknowledge the cross here on earth, then they'll acknowledge it when they get to Heaven and meet Jesus because they'll know then who He is. The followers use the scripture at Romans 14:11 that says, "every knee shall bow" and they say that it doesn't matter if you accept Jesus and bow to Him now or accept Him later when you realize at Heaven's door that He's God. Either way, you're saved and you'll bow to Him and once you do that, you're in Heaven.

Contrary to false doctrine, there is a "hell"! The Bible tells us in James 2:19 that even the devil believes in God—and yet he has been sentenced to hell. We also learn in Isaiah 5:14 that sinners will go to hell, and in Matthew 23:33 Jesus warns the Pharisees about hell. He also tells the story in Luke 16:20-31 of Lazarus and the rich man—who was in hell. Finally, in Matthew 25:41-46, we read how Jesus will judge the unsaved people and how they will be sentenced to hell along with the devil. It is sheer stupidity to not accept what the Bible says about hell, and it's foolish to refuse to believe that it exists just because we don't want to change our ways.

This new age doctrine is not the gospel of Jesus! It's not what Jesus preached, nor is it the gospel that Jesus inspired the apostles to preach, nor is it the gospel that He has instructed us to preach—Mark 16:15. If we are all automatically saved, then what is the purpose of the gospel of Jesus? Why does He tell us to preach it if we're all saved anyway? And what is the point in God inspiring men to write the scriptures if it's not necessary for us to know them?

Jesus said in Matthew 24:14 that this "gospel"—the gospel of Jesus—would be preached throughout the nations. He also instructed us in Mark 1:15, "Repent ye, and believe the gospel." Repent? The new-agers have missed that part. They feel that repentance isn't necessary; yet, the gospel of

Christ, as taught by the Lord Himself and by the apostles, says that repentance IS necessary for salvation.

Jesus said in Matthew 9:13 that He has "called sinners unto repentance", and in Luke 3:3 it says that Jesus was, "preaching the baptism of repentance for the remission of sins". Luke 15:7 further confirms the need for repentance when Jesus said, "I say unto you, that likewise joy shall be in heaven over one sinner that repenteth, more than over ninety and nine just persons, which need no repentance."

After Jesus was raised from the dead, He walked with His disciples and told them, as recorded in Luke 24:47, "Repentance and remission of sins should be preached in his name among all nations, beginning at Jerusalem." Also, Apostle Paul said in Acts 26:20 that, "...they should repent and turn to God, and do works meet for repentance." So now we see that the gospel message includes repentance and remission of sins.

Jesus paid for our sins, but it's not an automatic salvation. We must each come to Him on our own and repent and accept the pardon for our sins that He gave us at the cross, and then receive His new life in us—His Holy Spirit— and THEN we are born again; then we are saved from the judgment that comes to those who still have sin in them.

> Therefore if any man be in Christ, he is a new creature: old things are passed away; behold, all things are become new.—2 Corinthians 5:17

Jesus tells us in Luke 9:23 to pick up our cross and follow Him. This means that we cannot continue to live the way we did in the world because now we live for Him, not for the world. We are changed. We are filled with His spirit and we are different! We repented and left our sins at the foot of the cross and we left the sinful nature that was in us when we accepted our salvation.

We learn in Matthew 6:24 that we cannot serve two masters; we will love one and hate the other, but we cannot serve both. We also learn in 2 Corinthians 6:14 that when we are born again, we don't have anything in common with those who aren't. And Jesus warns us John 3:3, "Verily, verily, I say unto thee, 'Except a man be born again, he cannot see the kingdom of God'." So, we can't assume our salvation because as we see, we need to repent to have our sins forgiven so the old nature in us will die, and then we will be born again to receive His spirit and then we have the right to believe the promise of God that we will be with Jesus forever.

> To open their eyes, and to turn them from darkness to light, and from the power of Satan unto God, that they may receive forgiveness of sins, and inheritance among them which are sanctified by faith that is in me.—Acts 26:18

When we know God through His grace of salvation, we hear His voice as He speaks to us through the scriptures. John 10:27 says, "My sheep hear my voice, and I know them, and they follow me." When we were of the world, we only heard the voice of the spirit of the world. But now we hear His voice because His spirit is in us.

Jesus came to earth because He wanted to come— because He loves us enough to die for us. Apostle Peter tells us in 2 Peter 3:9 that it wasn't God's will for anyone to die— that's why He became the atonement for all mankind. Yet, not everyone will accept it and repent. The new age religions feel that they don't need to.

Apostle Paul teaches us in 2 Timothy 2:15 that we need to study the Bible so we can know Jesus and so we can become wise in the things of God and not be deceived by the false doctrines that hover around us. Too many Christians wander into these false religions because they seem to be right, but if they had studied the Bible and knew the truth, they would not have fallen prey to the deceptions of these false doctrines.

We cannot take a few scriptures and twist them to our convenience. The Inclusion doctrine does this and expects God to accept us as we are without the need to change or repent. But they are deceived and all those who follow will suffer the punishment of sin.

Let's not follow foolishness because we're lazy and want a short cut to our salvation. Let's get to Heaven through the door that Jesus has provided—John 10:7— and let's do it by repenting of our sins, turning away from them, and then being filled with His spirit so we can follow Him. Let's do it with a grateful heart and through obedience to His faithfulness of the cross!

> His lord said unto him, 'Well done, thou good and faithful servant: thou hast been faithful over a few things, I will make thee ruler over many things: enter thou into the joy of thy lord'.—Matthew 25:21

The Sorrow of Doing Nothing

There are many contentious issues debated in our world today that seem to divide even the Christians. Many believers will voice their opinion, but it's in secret or amongst themselves; they won't take a public stand for what is right. They don't realize that they are part of the problem when they just let things happen and say that it's the way of the world or that they weren't called to be preachers. This attitude does nothing to show the truth of God, and the results work against us because there is sorrow in doing nothing.

We are living in the last days before Christ's return and our King is soon going to be here! We cannot sit back and just wait for Him to arrive and let the world continue to destroy the people in it. It's heartless to not care about what will happen to them. We need to prepare them for this great event and that means telling them about Christ so they can repent of the sins and turn from this world so they can know Jesus and be saved from the wrath of God that's quickly coming upon this earth. We need to stop being the quiet Christian who doesn't want to stir the waters and become the Christian warrior that Jesus has called us to be. We need to get out there and point the people to God because it is not pleasing to Him that we do nothing. He is returning soon and we need to warn the people!

> When I say unto the wicked, Thou shalt surely die; and thou givest him not warning, nor speakest to warn the wicked from his wicked way, to save his life; the same wicked man shall die in his iniquity; but his blood will I require at thine hand. 19 Yet if thou warn the wicked, and he turn not from his wickedness, nor from his wicked way, he shall die in his iniquity; but thou hast delivered thy soul.—Ezekiel 3:18-19

Christians are partly responsible for some of the sins that our excelling in the world today. They didn't speak up when the various issues were proposed by the world, but instead, sat back and just let them happen. Many were disgusted and declared them to be wrong amongst themselves, but few people took a public stand and said, "NO! We won't allow this." The perfect example is the issue of abortion. If Christians had fought for the unborn child way back when it was first brought up, it might not have succeeded as a "legal" means to an end an innocent just because an unfortunate girl got herself pregnant out-of-wedlock. It just may have continued to be considered murder! But, Christians stayed silent and just let the world have its way.

Today we have several groups of pro-lifers who want to change the earthly laws and this is good because they are letting us know that it's wrong. Unfortunately, the time to make the greatest impact to stop it has passed and the world no longer looks at abortion as killing an innocent unborn baby; it looks at it as removing an unwanted fetus. And so, we have an epidemic of babies being murdered every day because the world made it legal and we did nothing to stop it.

Thou shalt not kill.—Exodus 20:13

We never fought hard enough when the world wanted to remove God from our public schools, and now we have more fear and violence against our children than we ever imagined possible. Not only are their lives at risk from individuals who decide to just shoot them dead, but our children are learning the way of the world and are being taught to accept immorality and religion apart from God as being the way of life. God has been removed. Now as we see the error of our way, many believers want to change the law to allow God back in—but it's too late. The world spoke louder than the Christians and now God has been legally

197

removed! Christians missed their opportunity to speak up and fight when the issues first began to circulate, and now our children and our future will reap the dangerous and evil benefits of our ignorance.

> Deliver me from mine enemies, O my God: defend me from them that rise up against me.—Psalm 59:1

Many people don't raise their children to know God and so they have no true benchmark to guide their lives. Others did teach them about God, but let them wonder off and accept the ways of the world. Discipline seems to be outdated as the new teaching is to let the child experience life and let them decide what is right and what is wrong. The children have been submitted to the world, and so now they are exposed only to the worldly teachers and to the social environment that no longer heeds to God and His laws. And many kids have no idea that God even exists or that one day He will judge them.

> Train up a child in the way he should go: and when he is old, he will not depart from it.— Proverbs 22:6

We can look around us at all the issues of life and see that God has been removed from most of them. Christians need to break out of the comfort zone and stand up and speak the truth even if it hurts! We need to follow the examples of Godly preachers like Billy Graham and Franklin Graham and speak out on God's behalf! We will be persecuted when we do this, but isn't it worth it? Isn't standing for the truth worth the glory that it brings to God? Isn't standing for what is right to save lives worth the effort? Shouldn't we defend the innocent and the young against the evil that controls this world and teach them about God who can save them? Surely, we don't want to face God and have Him say to us, "You didn't care enough to even try."

> For though I preach the gospel, I have nothing to glory of: for necessity is laid upon me; yea, woe is unto me, if I preach not the gospel!—1 Corinthians 9:16

It's not enough to just say that we are a Christian; we need to be one. Jesus tells us in Mark 8:34 to take up our cross and follow Him. He tells us in Mark 16:15 to preach the gospel and in Matthew 10:8 He tells us to help those in need and care for the poor and the sick. He doesn't tell us to leave it up to others to do; He tells us to get involved.

We can't all get out on the front lines to physically minister to people, but many of us can give our support financially to those who can. We can promote the issues on social networks and support those who are taking the various stands for God. And ALL of us can pray for God to intervene in these various issues. We can make it our daily regime to bring the issues before God, or some of us can even create prayer groups and get others to pray with us because we know God is present when two or three people pray together—Matthew 18:20. We can pray for change, pray for souls to be saved, and pray for laborers to get out there and let God work through them. We can pray for the peace of Jerusalem, that the Jewish people would come to know Jesus as their King so they, too, can be ready when He comes.

> Then saith He unto His disciples, 'The harvest truly is plenteous, but the labourers are few; 38 Pray ye therefore the Lord of the harvest, that He will send forth labourers into His harvest.'—Matthew 9:37-38

God tells us to occupy until He comes and that doesn't mean to just enjoy our life with all of its blessings; it also means to be busy working in His ministry in whatever capacity we can while there is still time.

A Christian who speaks for Christ and for the things of God has great power through the Holy Spirit to influence others and show them the way to God. We will all face Him one day, and how joyful that will be when we see how pleased He is with us for obeying Him and standing for His truth. How proud we'll be when we see souls in Heaven that we helped to bring there!

> Then shall the King say unto them on his right hand, 'Come, ye blessed of my Father, inherit the kingdom prepared for you from the foundation of the world: 35 For I was an hungered, and ye gave me meat: I was thirsty, and ye gave me drink: I was a stranger, and ye took me in: 36 Naked, and ye clothed me: I was sick, and ye visited me: I was in prison, and ye came unto me.' 37 Then shall the righteous answer him, saying, 'Lord, when saw we thee an hungered, and fed thee? or thirsty, and gave thee drink? 38 When saw we thee a stranger, and took thee in? or naked, and clothed thee? 39 Or when saw we thee sick, or in prison, and came unto thee?' 40 And the King shall answer and say unto them, 'Verily I say unto you, Inasmuch as ye have done it unto one of the least of these my brethren, ye have done it unto me.'—Matthew 25:34-40

Truth or Comfort Zone

Much of so-called "Christianity" today has digressed from the need of repentance that comes with a commitment to follow Christ, to an attitude of, "Jesus accepts us just as we are and we don't need to change to be saved." And sadly, this gives people a sense of spiritual security. It's a "new age religion" that says we can do our own thing and know that God loves and accepts each one of us just as we are now. It's no wonder that this "revival" is growing so rapidly! People believe that they don't have to read the scriptures to know God and are taught to simply listen to their "inner self" because that's God speaking to them. They believe that they don't have to change one sinful thing in their life to get into Heaven. But this is a blatant lie that will kill them! It is an anti-Christ spirit that says God will let anyone into Heaven without being saved. It's an attitude that is spreading because people want the blessings of God, and they don't realize that there is a difference between truth and a comfort zone.

Jesus tells us in Mark 12:30 that we are to love the Lord with all of our heart, mind, soul and strength. But how can we love God if we don't know Him? We can acknowledge His existence and we can speak kind things about Him, but unless we have a personal relationship with Him, we do not know Him. There is only one way to know God and that is to first accept Jesus as Lord and Savior, and then to read the Bible and learn about Him, about the love He has for His children, and about His ways, His values and His laws—and His judgment on those who rebel.

We aren't automatically born with our sins forgiven as this new age religion would have us believe. We need to obtain salvation by first learning what it is, why we need it and the fact that we're all guilty of sin—and we can only know this by reading the scriptures. Then we need to come to Jesus and ask Him to wash us clean in His blood because it was His shed blood that paid the price for our sins and made it possible for Him to forgive us. But it doesn't stop there. We also need to repent of all of our sins, accept His pardon for them and then turn away from them to follow Jesus.

> Then Peter said unto them, 'Repent, and be baptized every one of you in the name of Jesus Christ for the remission of sins, and ye shall receive the gift of the Holy Ghost.'— Acts 2:38

Only then are we born again, which means we have received the Holy Spirit in us to replace the spirit of the world that has been removed from us. Then and only then are we adopted or grafted into the family of God with the promise of being with Him throughout eternity.

> Therefore if any man be in Christ, he is a new creature: old things are passed away; behold, all things are become new.—2 Corinthians 5:17

> Jesus answered and said unto him, 'Verily, verily, I say unto thee, Except a man be born again, he cannot see the kingdom of God'.— John 3:3

> Being born again, not of corruptible seed, but of incorruptible, by the word of God, which liveth and abideth for ever.—1 Peter 1:23

The new thought for new age "Christians" is that God is a god of love—only, meaning that He loves everyone just as we are; that there is no need to change because He knows our faults and He's okay with them; that He does not punish or judge or condemn anyone because we were all forgiven at the cross whether we know it now or not. What a deception!

It's true that God does love everyone—and John 3:16 says so—but it also says that whoever believes on Him should not perish but would have everlasting life. Therefore, if we don't believe on Him, (don't accept that He died for our sins, and then repent and receive His salvation personally and get filled with His Spirit) then we will perish—as in face God on Judgment Day and stand before Him with all of our sins in us. And sin has its reward:

> For the wages of sin is death; but the gift of God is eternal life through Jesus Christ our Lord.—Romans 6:23

> I am He that liveth, and was dead; and, behold, I am alive for evermore, Amen; and have the keys of hell and of death.— Revelation 1:18

> And the sea gave up the dead which were in it; and death and hell delivered up the dead which were in them: and they were judged every man according to their works.— Revelation 20:13

So many people think that they're Christians, but they don't know Christ. So how can they believe in someone they don't know? Because if they knew Him, they'd also know that they need to come to Him and repent! But the new age religion doesn't believe in repentance because they feel they don't have any sin in them since Jesus died for everyone, and that when He said, "It is finished", it means there's nothing for us to do. How dangerous! God's redemption plan was finished at the cross, but we still need to repent and be forgiven.

If you're following a doctrine that says you don't need to repent, then you better read your Bible while you still can because it clearly says that every single person needs to come to Jesus and repent of their sins. Apostle Paul tells us in Romans 3:23 that all of us have sinned and come short of the glory of God.

> I came not to call the righteous, but sinners to repentance.—Luke 5:32

> I say unto you, that likewise joy shall be in heaven over one sinner that repents, more than over ninety and nine just persons, which need no repentance.—Luke 15:7

> And...If we say that we have no sin, we deceive ourselves, and the truth is not in us.— 1 John 1:8

People cannot create a god in their mind that fits their own sinful desires, ignore the Bible and not follow God's laws, and then think that they are actually serving the God of Heaven. They are serving a god, but it's the god of this world who has deceived them. They may feel "spiritual", but it's not God's Spirit that's leading them. And if these people would actually pray to God and read their Bibles, they would learn the truth. But they don't want to learn the truth because they don't want to change. They like the new-age version of Christ and don't want to be subjected to the rules in God's scriptures. But, there is danger in serving other gods and we've been warned that we are not to have any gods ahead of Jehovah God.

> Thou shalt have no other gods before me.— Exodus 20:3

We cannot serve a false god and expect good things to come of it, and we're walking a very dangerous line if we think we can. We cannot stay in our comfort zone and expect to be blessed by God; instead, we will face judgment. It would be like saying that we are an adopted child of an earthly family, yet we've never bothered to know them, nor do we care to do so. We never visit them, never call, never get involved with any of their concerns and issues, don't celebrate their accomplishments, don't cry over their sorrows and don't uphold their standards and values. Yet, we identify them by name and feel fully entitled to a massive inheritance from the parents when the will is read.

Salvation is God's redemption plan for everyone, and being filled with His Spirit is His gift to all who repent and accept it. God has done all He's going to do. It's up to us to accept it and follow Him or refuse it and face His judgment.

Have you repented and accepted His gift of life? Time is running out and you need to decide now whether you'll follow the truth or stay in your comfort zone. But don't take too long to decide—Jesus is getting ready to come back and it'll be too late to choose when you face Him.

> And if it seem evil unto you to serve the Lord, choose you this day whom ye will serve; whether the gods which your fathers served that were on the other side of the flood, or the gods of the Amorites, in whose land ye dwell: but as for me and my house, we will serve the Lord.—Joshua 24:15

Revival or Hype

The earth is being filled with "Christians". Some of these people are genuine, born-again believers, but many of them don't even know God. They are captivated by a doctrine that speaks of universal love and heavenly blessings, and the churches are filling up as people gather together to celebrate this new found freedom. And although few of these followers are saved or even know God, it's being called a revival because it is growing so fast. In fact, many people are looking at this massive growth in church attendance as being the greatest revival in history, but it's not a true gospel revival. People are being deceived and they are not able to discern between a real revival and hype.

A Christian revival happens when large numbers of people hear the gospel being preached over a short period of time and turn from the world to accept Christ's salvation. It involves preaching of the gospel and people repenting and giving their lives to Jesus—the Jesus of the Holy Bible—as we see in past revivals. What we have today is not a revival. The mega churches that are presented across the world are not all preaching the gospel and preparing us for the return of King Jesus. But rather, they are stoking the people through earthly lusts and desires, inspiring them through the riches of the leaders, and prompting them through music that stimulates their emotions. This is not what the gospel of Jesus is about. This a false gospel that's captivating millions of people into walking a fine line; one that is serving their own desires instead of seeking God's truth.

We are warned many times in the New Testament about these wolves who will come in the name of Jesus and deceive the people. We're told that there will be false prophets and teachers who will come to steal the people away from God through deception, and through earthly lusts.

Beware of false prophets, which come to you in sheep's clothing, but inwardly they are ravening wolves. 16 Ye shall know them by their fruits. Do men gather grapes of thorns, or figs of thistles? 17 Even so every good tree bringeth forth good fruit; but a corrupt tree bringeth forth evil fruit.—Matthew 7:15-17

And many false prophets shall rise, and shall deceive many.—Matthew 24:11

False prophets and teachers rob their followers of the truth about salvation and lead them through deception to the false doctrine that preaches of the blessings of God instead of the judgment to come. They become addicted to the fast-paced worship music that sings of their new life in Christ, rather than about the glory of God. They are stoked through this music because it leaves them emotionally high. Their faith lies dormant while they engage in works that they assume will lead them down the narrow path and through the Pearly Gates of Heaven.

However, emotions—how we feel and the temporary thrill from the music—have nothing to do with being saved! Salvation is given through faith, not through a feeling. We are saved when we hear preaching that convicts us of our sin and we repent to serve Christ. And this happens because God has given us a tiny seed of faith, just enough for us to believe God and come to the cross to accept the salvation of Jesus. Only faith will allow us to believe that God is our Heavenly Father and creator of the universe. Only faith will allow us to see that Jesus is His Son who came to earth and died for our sins, was buried and then raised from the dead to live evermore as our Lord and King. Happy emotions will never convict anyone of the truth; they just make us feel good.

> For by grace are ye saved through faith; and
> that not of yourselves: it is the gift of God.—
> Ephesians 2:8

It's really sad when people think they are Christians and actually expect to get into Heaven when they don't even know God. Yet, there are so many people out there who prefer to follow an easy, false doctrine about God rather than search the scriptures so they can know God and obey Him. Many of these people prefer to follow a leader who professes to know God, and they put their trust in this person and follow his (or her) instructions. And then when they join into the emotional worship at church, they think they are experiencing God's presence.

The only way anyone will experience God's presence is to know Him. And that begins with coming to the foot of the cross and laying down all of our sins at the cross and accepting His grace and forgiveness, and then turning away from our sinful life. But it doesn't stop there. We need to be filled with His Spirit and then study the scriptures—His words of instruction (the Bible)—so that we can know Him, because His Spirit in us will teach us the truth.

> Study to shew thyself approved unto God, a
> workman that needeth not to be ashamed,
> rightly dividing the word of truth.—2
> Timothy 2:15

Worship is good, and music is a perfect means to bring us into God's presence! God wants us to praise Him with music. And yes, it can become emotional as we pour praises out to the Lord, but our praises are to give glory to God and not to make us emotionally high. Our purpose is to seek God and to sing to Him alone. Our purpose is not to make ourselves feel good, but rather, to exalt God and give Him glory and honor.

> While I live will I praise the Lord: I will sing
> praises unto my God while I have any
> being.—Psalm 146:2

We walk a very thin and exceptionally dangerous line
when we try to live a "Christian" life our way and not
according to the Bible. Remember Cain? He didn't want to
offer God an offering that symbolized the atonement of
Christ; he wanted to do it his way—and he lost. There is only
one way to Heaven and that is through Christ.

> I am the door: by me if any man enter in, he
> shall be saved, and shall go in and out, and
> find pasture.—John 10:9

We can sing songs and even write our own songs and
promote them, but they are not worship songs unto the Lord
just because their hype makes us happy. We need to
recognize the difference between songs of worship that take
us into God's presence and songs of hype that sing about how
great we are because of God. Unless we know Him, and
unless those songs are from our heart to glorify God alone,
they are just songs. But the leaders of so many churches
promote these songs as worship songs and make the people
feel that they are accepted because they sing them. But these
songs don't make us a Christian; in fact, they help to keep us
from it because of the deception. To quote Keith Green,
"Going to church doesn't make you a Christian any more than
going to McDonald's makes you a hamburger."—(No
Compromise, the Life Story of Keith Green by Melody
Green and David Hazard; Sparrow Press, 1989)

Being a Christian means having faith in God and
accepting His salvation, and it means being able to praise
God whether we're happy or sad. It's not determined by our
emotions; our emotions are determined by our salvation. And

Ronnie Dauber

it's a thin line that we walk that will cause us to fall when we believe that we can get to Heaven our way.

> Jesus saith unto him, I am the way, the truth,
> and the life: no man cometh unto the Father,
> but by me.—John 14:6

Not All Bible Teachers Know God

No matter where we go today, whether it's church, a Christian gathering or social media, we encounter at least so-called Christian who feels that they deserve our uttermost respect because they have diligently studied the scriptures and their knowledge makes them superior to the rest of us. The irony, of course, is that anyone can study the Bible from Genesis to Revelation and become fully educated in its "logic". But unfortunately, logic will not save us; nor will it lead us to the heart of God. We need to be careful who we follow because he or she may consider themselves educated, but it does not mean that they know God.

And while the merits of their knowledge can be a blessing to us at times, we need to be careful that we don't become followers of these teachers instead of followers of God. We need to study the Bible ourselves and let God teach us rather than depend on someone just because they claim to know it all. And we can never allow these people to manipulate our lives to the point where we begin to question our own walk with God. What we do need to do is study the Bible prayerfully and let God's Spirit teach us His truth.

> Study to shew thyself approved unto God, a workman that needeth not to be ashamed, rightly dividing the word of truth.—2 Timothy 2:15

Theologians today are comparable to the scribes we learn about in the New Testament. These are the people who knew the words of the scriptures because their job was to make copies of the original transcripts. (They did this by hand since our convenience of technology wasn't developed at that time, and so it was intense and required a lot of their time.) Many of them loved God, but just as many became theologians for the knowledge of the scriptures, not because they wanted to know or love God.

> For I say unto you, 'That except your righteousness shall exceed the righteousness of the scribes and Pharisees, ye shall in no case enter into the kingdom of heaven.'— Matthew 5:20

We learn from their approach and attitude towards Jesus that they were filled with the knowledge, but had no heartfelt revelation of the truth. In other words, they were fully educated in the scriptures, but lacked in love and commitment to God because the words of the scriptures never went from their educated minds into their heart. They didn't recognize that Jesus was the promised Messiah, and when some began to put it together through the crowds who followed our Lord, they denied who He was and wouldn't even humble themselves before Him. They considered themselves to be above everyone else because they were a small minority who had full knowledge of the scriptures.

They were scribes. They knew it all. They were puffed up in their minds and demanded the respect of the people, and they bowed down to no one. And many theologians today are exactly the same. Their desire is to make themselves more knowledgeable through studying, rather than to be humbled with a heart of servitude towards God. And this can be extremely dangerous because as close as they are to His words, they don't know Him.

> From that time forth began Jesus to shew unto His disciples, how that He must go unto Jerusalem, and suffer many things of the elders and chief priests and scribes, and be killed, and be raised again the third day.— Matthew 16:21

They love to debate sections of scripture, but let anyone challenge their knowledge and some of them will get outright angry and even cruel towards those who dared to question them. And sadly, some even use words that are shocking for so-called Christians. These theologians are not up to correction at all, and they certainly don't appreciate anyone adding anything to their conclusions. They believe that they are better than the rest of us and they inadvertently demand our submission to them.

And while it's always good to respect someone who knows more than we do, it's not acceptable that they think they have the right to demand it or to put us down publically because they didn't get that respect! What many of them fail to realize is that Christians are ALL saved by grace, that we have ALL sinned and that when we come to Jesus and repent, He forgives us ALL of us and fills us with His Holy Spirit. They miss the fact that when we are saved, we are ALL equal to each other in God's eyes, and that as brethren we are to encourage and support each other.

> For all have sinned, and come short of the glory of God.—Romans 3:23

> Charity suffereth long, and is kind; charity envieth not; charity vaunteth not itself, is not puffed up.—1 Corinthians 13:4

When we study the scriptures prayerfully, God's Holy Spirit teaches us the truth—the revelation behind the words in the Bible. We can read about who Jesus is and we can use logic to agree with it all, but unless it's in our heart it means nothing! We are not saved because of what we know; we are saved because of what we believe!

> That if thou shalt confess with thy mouth the Lord Jesus, and shalt believe in thine heart

that God hath raised Him from the dead, thou
shalt be saved.—Romans 10:9

And if we believe and accept that Jesus is the Son of
God who came to earth, died on the cross for our sins, was
raised on the third day, lives forever more as our Lord and
Savior and is about to return to earth again as our King, then
we are saved. We study the Bible because we want to know
God and He will teach us as we go. We will gradually
become like Jesus, bearing the same fruits as Jesus and
having the same love for others that He has for us. We will
become more knowledgeable in the scriptures, but our heart
will grow in leaps and bounds and we will illuminate God's
love everywhere we go because He is leading us. We are not
leading ourselves because of who we think we are; we are
letting Jesus lead us because of who we KNOW Jesus is.

When we love God we also love the brethren. We
don't belittle or berate anyone just because they don't know
or understand what we do. But rather, we love others because
we know that we all belong to God and that He died for all of
us. Someone who studies the scriptures for knowledge may
be well educated in them for facts and logic, but those who
humbly study so they can know God will be taught His truth
through the Holy Spirit and will become wise!

Beloved, let us love one another: for love is of
God; and every one that loveth is born of
God, and knoweth God.8 He that loveth not
knoweth not God; for God is love.—1 John
4:7-8

We need to examine ourselves and if we see that we
are at the point where we feel we know it all and that we are
above correction, that's when we need to stop because we
have missed the mark completely! We need to turn around,

go back to where we left Jesus and repent—and then allow Him to teach us and guide us through the scriptures!

And if we don't know Jesus, then we need to repent, ask Him to forgive us and fill us with His Spirit so that we can know beyond a shadow of a doubt that we are saved! And then we can study the scriptures with a totally different viewpoint—revelation from God.

> Not everyone that saith unto me, 'Lord, Lord', shall enter into the kingdom of heaven; but he that doeth the will of my Father which is in heaven. 22 Many will say to me in that day, Lord, Lord, have we not prophesied in thy name? and in thy name have cast out devils? and in thy name done many wonderful works? 23 And then will I profess unto them, I never knew you: depart from me, ye that work iniquity.—Matthew 7:21-23

We live in a world that is plagued with darkness, and sometimes it gets very difficult to see the Light, especially when we allow ourselves to be entangled with "scribes" whose hearts aren't set on serving God, but rather, are on boasting in their own glory. God has given us His Spirit who lives in us, and as we study the scriptures with a humble heart so we can know Him and serve Him better, we will be able to do all that Jesus has called us to do. And we will do it all to the glory of God!

> Wherefore receive ye one another, as Christ also received us to the glory of God.— Romans 15:7

Be Doers and Not Just Hearers

We can't help but notice that the world is in a mess! From domestic issues to worldly disasters, it appears as if everything is coming undone at the seams. While we can't control most of it, we can't just ignore it, either. There are things we can do as Christians that will not only help others get through it, but will allow God to work through us and show His love to a hurting world. Being a Christian is more than just attending church and seeking out blessings; it's reaching out to others and extending God's love to them!

We Can Speak Out!

We can't all be the ones to lead crusades against sins such as abortion, but we can speak to individuals, in small groups and in the social media sites online. We see posts coming down the timelines and many of us won't pass that post on because we don't want to cause conflict amongst our own friends. But we should value the laws of God much higher than the opinions of others. We should make the issue of murdering unborn children more important than our own persona. These media sites are our opportunity to speak up and declare that murder is wrong. It's our chance to touch the lives and influence them with God's truth, that abortion is murder and a sin against God. It just might touch someone and save a life!

> Lo, children are a heritage of the Lord: and the fruit of the womb is his reward.—Psalm 127:3

We Can Support the Missionaries!

We're not all called to work as missionaries, but most of us can afford a few dollars a month to support those who are called. This provides food and medical care for the precious, hurting people who need it so desperately. It also enables the missionaries to keep working, AND it gives them the supplies and equipment to teach them about Jesus. And all of us have the ability to pray for the missionaries in these countries and ask God to meet all of their needs. What an amazing way to show the love of God to those who are searching for Him!

> And the King shall answer and say unto them, 'Verily I say unto you, Inasmuch as ye have done it unto one of the least of these my brethren, ye have done it unto me.'—Matthew 25:40

We Can Get Involved in Politics!

Politics is a touchy subject, but we need to get involved. We can't all be part of the governing political agencies, but we can pray that God will raise up mighty men and women who will serve Him and who will fight for the rights of Christians. We can be part of petitions that declare we want God back in our schools, and we can proclaim our right to read the Bible in public. Many of us could work voluntarily with some local offices and others could support them financially. We are entitled to the freedom that our country was founded on and we need to get involved to bring that freedom back. We need to continue to preach the gospel of Christ so people can be saved and escape the judgment that will soon come upon our country because our government has chosen to remove God from the people.

> For the eyes of the Lord are over the righteous, and His ears are open unto their prayers: but the face of the Lord is against them that do evil.—1 Peter 3:12

We Can Become Doers, not Hearers Only!

The world is suffering from natural disasters, wars and horrendous religious attacks against communities, and there are teams of workers who go out to help the people restore their lives in the aftermath. Some of us can help by working hands-on in local areas or even in distant areas, but most of us can't. But we can send our financial support to reputable groups such as Samaritan's Purse that sends out teams around the world to help the people in these disasters. We cannot allow the tainted reputation of worldly organizations to prohibit us from helping Christian organizations that work to the glory of God. We can work, pray, encourage or support those who are trying to bring life back to these devastated communities.

> For I was an hungered, and ye gave me meat: I was thirsty, and ye gave me drink: I was a stranger, and ye took me in: 36 Naked, and ye clothed me: I was sick, and ye visited me: I was in prison, and ye came unto me.— Matthew 25:35-36

We can be a Responsible Parent!

Many of us have raised our children in the church, but some of these children have wandered away and no longer serve God. As parents, we need to lift them up to God in prayer constantly because God hears our prayers and He loves these children even in their rebellious times. We must stay strong and let our testimony and love towards them be our greatest tool, outside of prayer. We can't approve of the wrong in their lives, but we can always be there for them in love so they will eventually see the error of their ways and return to God.

Many others became Christians after their children were raised in the world and these children don't know God. We need to keep them in prayer constantly and live honestly before God as a testimony to the children. Our actions and reactions, our words, our values, the way we present ourselves and the way we treat others will be a witness to them. We try to teach them about God and the love of Jesus, and we get involved with them in prayer, reading and singing whenever possible, and we don't allow the enemy to discourage us through their negative words and actions. Instead, we cling to God and His promises.

> Train up a child in the way he should go: and
> when he is old, he will not depart from it.—
> Proverbs 22:6

We can Care for the Elderly!

Many of us have elderly loved ones living in a long-term care facility because of age and medical conditions. Too often these precious people feel that they've been deserted and forgotten. They can't speak for themselves, but they hurt and they crave for our love and attention. We can't let their physical and mental state replace who they were and who they still are. They are still worthy of our love and respect. They may seem difficult and challenging, even nasty at times, but beneath this torment is someone we love and we must never ignore them—or worse, resent them because they've changed. The facility can care for them physically, but it can't provide the love they need or get rid of the hurt they suffer as they come to grips with the fact that they can't be themselves. They don't appreciate the physical care they're getting nearly as much as they feel the love when we visit them and show that we care.

> Hearken unto thy father that begat thee, and
> despise not thy mother when she is old.—
> Proverbs 23:22

We Can Pray for the sick!

219

Ronnie Dauber

Many people suffer from sickness and disease and then succumb to whatever the medical profession deals them. Whether it's a long-term, permanent, or a life-threatening disease, it is horrendous for the person who has to endure it. Whatever it is, we can take it to God in prayer and trust Him to help them through it. We can encourage them to study the Bible and trust God because He said He would heal us if we ask. And sometimes that healing requires us to turn away from the medical world and let God's natural medicines heal. God healed us at the cross and we need to be the light to these ill people and encourage them to keep their faith in Him. Some won't survive even with prayers, but God can heal their heart so they can know that they have a home waiting for them in Heaven.

> But He was wounded for our transgressions, He was bruised for our iniquities: the chastisement of our peace was upon Him; and with His stripes we are healed.—Isaiah 53:5

Many of us are not able to be on the front lines of the many battles that people fight in this world, but most of us can do something. We need to do something. We can no longer just sit and watch and hope. James 2:20 says that faith without works is dead, so let's put our faith to work and do something. Let's not keep silent because we're worried that we'll cause a scene. Let's make a noise! Let's take a stand for God today and let's be a blessing to others!

> And the King shall answer and say unto them, 'Verily I say unto you, Inasmuch as ye have done it unto one of the least of these my brethren, ye have done it unto me.'—Matthew 25:40

Hiding Your Talents

It's surprising to learn just how many Christians are silent about their faith and feel that it's not their calling to preach the gospel. And while it's true that we aren't all called to be preachers, we can't ignore our own responsibilities. Every Christian has been given at least one talent—and for a reason—and God expects us to use that talent. One day we will each stand before Christ as He asks us what we did with that talent. What will you tell Him?

We know that all the disciples of Jesus were called by Him to preach the gospel to the Jewish nation first and then to the Gentiles, and yet we read about the teachings and experiences of some more than we do of others. They were equally loved and valued by God, but He gave greater responsibilities—more talents—to some of them, just as He gives different measures of talents to us today.

> And unto one He gave five talents, to another two, and to another one; to every man according to his several ability; and straightway took his journey.—Matthew 25:15

Apostle Paul was given more "talents" than any of the other apostles, but that also meant that God required more from him. His rewards in Heaven would be greater, but so would his responsibilities and challenges be greater here on earth. As the saying goes, "with much privilege comes much responsibility".

> For unto whomsoever much is given, of him shall be much required: and to whom men have committed much, of him they will ask the more.—Luke 12:48

And it is a privilege to be called to do something for the Lord—to do anything for the Lord. We look at devoted and faithful preachers like Rev. Billy Graham and we say, "I could never do that." And most of us couldn't, but God knew Rev. Graham's heart and He knew that He could trust him to do the job He gave him to do—to use the talents He gave him. Rev. Graham has publically admitted many times that he loved that God had called him to preach, but that he had no idea at that time of the extent of his calling. Yet, this didn't stop this man from pushing forward because His heart was for God and God gave him the ability to do the job. And even in his old age, Billy Graham remains faithful.

We know of many other Godly men and women who spend their lives sharing the gospel and working in some area of the ministry for the Lord, and again we say that we could never do that. And most of us couldn't because that may not be what God wants us to do. Some Christians feel that if they had the money or if they were famous then they could be like those notable ones, but that is a weak excuse for choosing disobedience. Our mission is not to compare ourselves to anyone except to Jesus, and whatever He calls us to do should be an honor on our part to do.

> I press toward the mark for the prize of the high calling of God in Christ Jesus.—
> Philippians 3:14

Too many Christians forget that they are not doing anything for God on their own merits or abilities. God is not weak. He isn't stumped or stopped because someone wouldn't answer His call. He'll get someone else to do it and deal with the one who wouldn't obey Him later—as on Judgment Day if that person doesn't repent.

God will give us the ability to do it! He will supply our needs to do the job and He will meet all the challenges that come against us because He wants the truth to get out there while there is still time. He wants people to turn away from their sinful life and come to Him. He loves us and doesn't want anyone to face His wrath and be judged because of the sin that is found in them. He wants us to preach the gospel so people will turn away from their sin and follow Him. That's why He came to earth and took our sins to the cross—so we wouldn't have to endure the punishment for them ourselves.

However, many of us have no idea what God wants us to do and so we either choose to do our own thing and hope it works, or we do nothing. And many Christians are comfortable just attending church services, staying separate from the rest of the world and doing nothing. Unfortunately, this doesn't mean that they are being totally obedient to God just because they don't fellowship with unbelievers. Jesus commissioned us all to preach the gospel, and because He loves us He will equip us with whatever it takes to do the job. We wouldn't send our own child outdoors in winter to shovel the driveway without first making sure he was dressed for the weather and had the equipment to do the job. And God doesn't send out His children to do jobs without giving them what they need, either.

Inside each of us is a talent (or maybe several talents) that needs to be used and we need to find it and do something with it. Doing nothing isn't an option.

> And He said unto them, 'Go ye into all the world, and preach the gospel to every creature.'—Mark 16:15

There is something that each of can do. Perhaps it's to write Christian articles or blogs, or to sing or write music, or to simply be an outgoing encouragement to others. Possibly it's to financially support a Christian ministry. Maybe it's to open our home for prayer meetings or to be a prayer warrior! Maybe it's to create artwork to share and inspire others, or maybe it's to read stories to kindergarten children, or even to answer phones at a call-in center of some ministry. Perhaps it's to volunteer a few hours a week at an old age home or sick children's hospital. Maybe it's to be a friendly, helpful neighbor who is always ready to give a helping hand and who brings joy and inspiration to those around.

Regardless of what we think we can or cannot do, we have something in each of us that God has given to us so that we can share the love of God with others. We should never look at the size of the gift or even at our own abilities because God will give us the ability and the strength to use it, to His glory.

When we come to God in prayer about this, some of us will be inspired by a great desire within that we can't ignore. It may be something very small at first, but it will grow and become the fulfillment of God's purpose for us when we are obedient and put that talent even in its early stage to work. And if we don't have a clue as to what our talent or talents are, then we need to ask God because He is faithful and He will answer our prayer.

> Ask, and it will be given to you; seek, and you will find; knock, and it will be opened to you. 8 For everyone who asks receives, and he who seeks finds, and to him who knocks it will be opened.—Matthew 7:7-8 NKJV

> But my God shall supply all your need according to his riches in glory by Christ Jesus.—Philippians 4:19

Few of us will ever be notorious for what we do, but all of us will be blessed by God for using what He has given to us to help save the souls of others and to be a blessing to those around us. We should never get lazy or assume that God hasn't got something very specific for us to do. We can't just hide our talents and then pretend we don't have any. We belong to Jesus, and the time to get out there and get souls saved will soon be gone. His spirit lives in us and the only way the people of the world will see God is through us! So let's be obedient to God and let's use our talents to show the love of God and the salvation of Jesus to a lost world!

> Let your light so shine before men, that they may see your good works, and glorify your Father which is in heaven.—Matthew 5:16

The Value of Your Life

Too often we base our actual human value—our true self-worth—on what we can do. While knowledge, expertise, experience and accomplishments add honor to our lifestyle, none of them depict our actual worth. They reveal what is important to us, what allows us to earn large paychecks and what makes us happy, but are the things we do the defining benchmark that makes our life valuable? How can we know what our life is really worth is if it's not through what we do?

What measures our value?

Our "worth" can't be measured by what we have earned or accomplished. If it was, then those people who have the same desire to serve but who lack the opportunity to do so would be worth much less than the one who lucked out and accomplished these feats. It's not practical to say that our worth as a person should be evaluated by our diplomas or certificates because there are many intelligent and skilled people who have the same knowledge and desires, just not the final documents to prove it. And their help in a time of need would prove to be just as valuable.

This doesn't mean that the works we do with our skills are not valuable to God; He wants us to use our talents, but it does mean that He treasures something within us far greater! And that is our heart because what we do reflects what's in our heart, and it's our heart that is valuable to God.

> When a man's ways please the Lord, He maketh even his enemies to be at peace with him.—Proverbs 16:7

God created people because He wanted a family to share His perfect life with. But He didn't want anyone in it this family that was there just for the benefits or just because it was the better of two choices. God wants people to be part

226

of His family because they love Him, and they love the life that He's made for them.

When Adam and Eve were in the garden, she was tempted by the devil and he disobeyed God. Then God separated Himself from them because they were no longer pure; they had been infiltrated with sin. And since God is Holy, anything that comes in His presence that isn't holy would be instantly destroyed. God loved Adam and Eve, as He loves all of His children, and He didn't want His family to be destroyed. He wanted them brought back so He could fellowship with them again.

So, Jesus came to earth to become a man, live amongst the people and teach them about God. His ultimate purpose was to give His life on the cross so He could take on the sins of all mankind and pay the punishment of death for those sins. This sacrifice is the greatest gift that any person can or will ever receive. He gave His life to save ours; this makes our life worth more than we can even imagine!

> For the wages of sin is death; but the gift of God is eternal life through Jesus Christ our Lord.—Romans 6:23

The entire Old Testament is about the coming of Jesus the Messiah, the one who would take the punishment for the sins of the people and restore them back to God, holy and sanctified through His own shed blood—(read Isaiah chapter 53).

> For God sent not His Son into the world to condemn the world; but that the world through Him might be saved.—John 3:14 (14-17)

When we look at the world around us, we see the corruption, the deception and the immorality that is plaguing the entire populous and we have to wonder why God did it. Why did He bother to fulfill His plan of redemption? Of the billions of people ever born, majority of them want nothing to do with Him. So why did He bother to leave His throne in Heaven, take on the form of a man, live on this earth without any material possessions besides the clothes on his back, and then endure the brutal torture and beatings that led to His horrific crucifixion on the cross, if most of the people don't care? Why? Because the soul of every single person ever born was worth the sacrifice to God!

> The Lord is not slack concerning his promise, as some men count slackness; but is longsuffering to us-ward, not willing that any should perish, but that all should come to repentance.—2 Peter 3:9

God knew that most people would reject Him and mock Him and refuse to associate with Him, but their soul was worth dying for anyway. God has always wanted everyone to see Him as the God of Heaven who loves them. The devil is God's enemy. People were never His enemy; they were His family. His love is first toward the Jews because they are the seed of Abraham who God promised He'd care for, equally with the Gentiles who are adopted into His family through the salvation of Christ.

To God, every soul was worth dying for and every soul was worth the beatings He took on our behalf. When He created us, He gave eternal value to each one of our souls, which means we will never die! God made us in His image— soul, spirit and body—and although we will get new bodies when we graduate to Heaven, our soul will never change because it's pure; it has been washed and cleansed in the blood of Jesus.

The righteous (those who accept the salvation of Jesus) will live eternally with God, the One who created them and who also saved them from their sins. Those who refuse to come to Him and accept His sacrifice will go to hell when they die, and will eventually be condemned to the Lake of Fire with the very devil who kept them from the true God of Heaven. It isn't God's will that they go there! But everyone will stand before Him one day and be judged *by* the law. If sin is found in them, they will have to pay the punishment for those sins. Jesus offered them a pardon, but they refused it.

> The Lord is not slack concerning his promise, as some men count slackness; but is longsuffering to us-ward, not willing that any should perish, but that all should come to repentance.—2 Peter 3:9

Our lives are worth everything to God and He loves each and every one of us, but not everyone loves Him. He doesn't take pleasure in punishing anyone to hell, but the sin in people will cause them to be judged by God's laws. Just as any person who commits a crime on earth would be judged by our earthly laws and sentenced to prison, God's laws judge and condemn every sin-filled soul to eternal prison.

So regardless of our talents, education, finances, abilities or disabilities, our lives are equally precious to God! Jesus left His throne in Heaven to come to earth so He could take on our sins and have us all pardoned from them so we wouldn't be found guilty of sin and punished for them when we stand before Him on Judgment Day. Truly, this reveals what we are worth to Him—we are worth dying for!

> Greater love hath no man than this, that a man [Jesus] lay down His life for His friends.— John 15:13

God as our Last Resort

Often when those unexpected trials and challenges come, many Christians will first try to work it out on their own or with the help of the world—and then when all else fails they'll turn to God. He is often the last resort people go to for help and *that* is a true sign that they have a situation even greater than their current problem! And that is that God is not first in their life when He is the last One they go to for help.

God should never be the last one we talk to about our problems. He should always be the very first one. But many "Christians" put God up on a pedestal and ignore Him like some forgotten king who they pay homage to on Sunday mornings and during special Christian events. Many prefer to avoid dealing with God altogether and choose to answer to a human leader, while others have just never bothered to know Him because they feel that they're saved and that's enough. These "so called" Christians feel that there is no need to have a personal relationship with God How can we call ourselves a Christian and not want to know God?

God is greater than the human mind can imagine and only someone who knows Him intimately will see Him for who He is and worship Him in everything they do! And that includes talking to Him first about their problems. When we realize that we are God's children, we ought to talk to Him about everything, and certainly He should be the first One who we cry out to for help.

> The Lord is my rock, and my fortress, and my deliverer; my God, my strength, in whom I will trust; my buckler, and the horn of my salvation, and my high tower.—Psalm 18:2

When an earthly family is closely knitted together, the children will share all of their joys and their sorrows with

230

their brothers and sisters AND with their parents. And when any of them face situations that are overwhelming, where they need help for something, the children will go to their father first with the full expectation that he will be the one most likely to get them through their crisis.

But sadly, many earthly families are not devoted to each other, and over the years the children have become estranged from their parents. They don't have that bonding or that devotion toward them as they should. So when a situation arises where one of the children needs help for whatever reason, it's very likely that the father would be the last person they would go to for help. Why? Because there is no love relationship between the children and the parents, and no trust or respect given to the parents.

This is also the problem with so-called Christians; they don't know their Heavenly Father and only acknowledge His distant existence. They are like the estranged child and so they put their trust in the world instead of in Him. They have remained at a distance and with an attitude of equality that doesn't allow them to become humble before Him.

When we become a Christian, we see Jesus as our Saviour, our Lord and our King, and we have the promise that one day Jesus will return to earth to rule over it as King. He's not here in person yet, but He's coming—and very soon! We know He's our king now and so we trust Him with our lives, but many won't realize it until they face Him on Judgment Day. And although they will bow to Him, it will be too late to accept His salvation then.

> For it is written, 'As I live', saith the Lord, 'every knee shall bow to me, and every tongue shall confess to God'.—Romans 14:11

Definition of a king: The Merriam-Webster dictionary defines king this way:

—a male monarch of a major territorial unit; especially one whose position is hereditary and who rules for life—a paramount chief— one that holds a preeminent position; especially: a chief among competitors

The Bible teaches that Jesus IS king over all the earth:

For unto us a child is born, unto us a son is given: and the government shall be upon his shoulder: and his name shall be called Wonderful, Counsellor, The mighty God, The everlasting Father, The Prince of Peace.— Isaiah 9:6

Now when Jesus was born in Bethlehem of Judaea in the days of Herod the king, behold, there came wise men from the east to Jerusalem, 2 Saying, 'Where is he that is born King of the Jews? for we have seen his star in the east, and are come to worship him'.— Matthew 2:1-2

Pilate therefore said unto Him, 'Art thou a king then?' Jesus answered, 'Thou sayest that I am a king. To this end was I born, and for this cause came I into the world, that I should bear witness unto the truth. Every one that is of the truth heareth my voice'.—John 18:37

The Merriam-Webster's dictionary describes a kingdom as:

—a country whose ruler is a king or queen— the spiritual world of which God is king

So when we, the citizens of God's kingdom, have an issue about anything, we should take it to our King first because we know that He will defend His citizens, provide our needs and care for us as children. We shouldn't take our problems to the outside world because we have no relationship with the world. We don't belong to the world. We should never want to show any disloyalty to our King because we know that He is the One who died to save us because He loves us, and if He'll do that, then He surely will help us with our problems.

Therefore, as a Christian—[a person who is saved by the blood of Jesus and has been born again into the family of God] we would automatically go to God because He is our king and He loves us and He does care for us. We should have confidence in God to protect us, help us, heal us and give us everything we need to overcome our problems.

God may use others to help us through our issues, but we trust Him and accept who He sends across our path. But if we choose the world over God and yet confess to be a Christian, we need to truly evaluate our life. Why? Because no one can serve two gods. It's either the God of Heaven or the god of this world.

> No man can serve two masters: for either he
> will hate the one, and love the other; or else
> he will hold to the one, and despise the other.
> Ye cannot serve God and mammon.—
> Matthew 6:24

So when a person makes God their last resort for help—or for anything, for that matter—it's because he or she doesn't know God, and doesn't worship Him and honor Him in everything they do. If they knew Him, and knew the price He paid to get them saved from the judgment that lies ahead, they would love Him with all their heart, mind, soul and strength—[Luke 10:27]. It doesn't matter if they call themselves Christians or not; if their heart isn't connected to God's heart, then they are deceived and sadly, they are NOT a Christian.

That person needs to repent, turn away from the sinful world and accept the salvation that Jesus has given to them through His own shed blood. And they need to make Him alone their King and Lord over their life. And then they'll know God and be over comers.

> These things I have spoken unto you, that in me ye might have peace. In the world ye shall have tribulation: but be of good cheer; I have overcome the world.—John 16:33

When God becomes our reason for living, He also becomes the One to whom we give all of our love and respect AND trust. And when we face any challenges in life, HE will be the first One we cry out to because we know that He loves us and will take care of us, just as He promised.

> Humble yourselves therefore under the mighty hand of God, that He may exalt you in due time: 7 Casting all your care upon Him; for He careth for you—1 Peter 5:6

Empty Batteries

The most important decision we will ever make in life is to accept the salvation of Christ. Many of us are zealous and unstoppable when we first get saved, but then the enthusiasm begins to fade away and the thrill of redemption soon becomes a lost moment in time. It's as if the whole event was triggered by hyped-up batteries that have slowly run out of energy.

Many people feel that when they get saved it's a one-time deal and will last forever, and so they never go beyond that initial acceptance. But what they forget, or perhaps don't even know, is that the gift of faith is a seed that they received to enable them to see a little glimpse of the truth about God, but it didn't give them instant knowledge or wisdom or insight to everything about God. It was just the beginning. They need to take that seed and plant it so it will grow into a wonderful relationship with God. Without this initial gift of faith, none of us would even care to know Him because God is Holy and sin is evil and the two don't mix.

> No man can serve two masters: for either he will hate the one, and love the other; or else he will hold to the one, and despise the other. Ye cannot serve God and mammon.— Matthew 6:24

This initial gift of faith is like a battery. It needs to be recharged over and over and over again in order for us to get the fullness of its use through its power. Batteries that require recharging will often get recharged when the person owning them sees that they're getting low in energy. Other people will simply let the batteries run low and forget about them and just assume that they're still loaded. And still others have batteries that were never recharged and they completely died so that there's no juice left in them to be recharged.

235

Faith is like a battery. Many people think that the initial charge will last forever, but it loses its strength when it's forgotten, and we need to recharge it often or it will die.

> Therefore hear the parable of the sower: 19 When anyone hears the word of the kingdom, and does not understand it, then the wicked one comes and snatches away what was sown in his heart. This is he who received seed by the wayside. 20 But he who received the seed on stony places, this is he who hears the word and immediately receives it with joy; 21 yet he has no root in himself, but endures only for a while. For when tribulation or persecution arises because of the word, immediately he stumbles. 22 Now he who received seed among the thorns is he who hears the word, and the cares of this world and the deceitfulness of riches choke the word, and he becomes unfruitful. 23 But he who received seed on the good ground is he who hears the word and understands it, who indeed bears fruit and produces: some a hundredfold, some sixty, some thirty.— Matthew 13:18-23 NKJV

It's sad that people will come to the cross, see Jesus for who He is and accept the salvation that He's given to them, but then so quickly return to the world they know and forget about that revelation. How can they just return to the world and forget it as if it never happened? Likely because they accepted the concept of salvation, but didn't accept Christ into their heart. Therefore, it's easy to forget. It was a great idea at the time, but there was not enough power or heartfelt desire in their (faith battery) heart to keep it going.

Once we know Jesus, it's almost impossible to turn away from Him. His love floods our being and we want more of Him. It seems almost contradictory to say this when we know that Judas Iscariot knew Jesus personally and still, he betrayed Him. Unfortunately, Judas loved money more than he loved God, and so when he turned against Jesus, knowing full well who He was, Judas committed the unpardonable sin. It's one thing to not know Jesus and not honor Him, but it's quite another to know Him and then turn against Him and choose to serve Satan instead. He didn't let his "batteries" run out. He deliberately threw them out.

> But, behold, the hand of him that betrayeth me is with me on the table. 22 And truly the Son of man goeth, as it was determined: but woe unto that man by whom he is betrayed!— Luke 22:21-22

When we get saved, we are forgiven for all of our sins because we accept that Jesus took them away from us when He died on the cross, and we accept that He gave us eternal life when He rose from the dead. But we can't assume that this revelation will remain a priority in our mind or in our heart if we don't do something to ensure it. We need to pray, study and worship! (PSW) Our worldly knowledge and experiences, friends and family influences, habits and desires will soon take over our life again if we don't make God a priority! It's easy to lose what God gave us if we don't take care of it. We need to make PSW part of our daily regime.

> Let the words of my mouth, and the meditation of my heart, be acceptable in thy sight, O Lord, my strength, and my redeemer.—Psalm 19:14

We need to fill our mind with the scriptures so that we can know Him, and then word-by-word we can push the world out of us. It's especially important and crucial to new believers to study the Bible prayerfully and let the Holy Spirit turn the words into revelation. When we commit our walk with God to a person—a preacher or a televangelist or even a friend—we risk learning a compromised version of God's truth. It's good that we get counsel and it's good that we find a church that preaches the unadulterated gospel of Christ, but it's even better to study the scriptures on our own and let God teach us the truth through His Spirit.

> This book of the law shall not depart out of thy mouth; but thou shalt meditate therein day and night, that thou mayest observe to do according to all that is written therein: for then thou shalt make thy way prosperous, and then thou shalt have good success. —Joshua 1:8

Our initial gift of faith is recharged every time we pray, study the Bible, and worship God. Our faith is like a battery; if we don't recharge it, it will die. A battery can get really low and almost empty, but if we get to it in time it can still be still recharged even if it's got only a bit of juice in it. However, a battery that has gone dead is just that; it's dead and can't be recharged. And when this happens we need to buy a new one. So when people lose the first battery—that first gift of faith—we need to pray that God will give them a second one, a second opportunity to come to the cross and accept Jesus as their Lord and Savior.

Does this mean that if someone comes to the cross and then just lets that special gift wear out that they can simply wait for the next opportunity to get saved? It's not that easy. If that person wanted to know God or felt that it was important to know Him, he would have fed that seed of faith and let it grow. But if he just let it pass, then God means nothing to him and he could still die lost. This is where the prayers of Christians will open doors for another opportunity. God says in 2 Peter 3:9 that He doesn't want anyone to perish. He will send different people and more opportunities to that person because one of them just may spark the person's heart and light it up.

However, no one knows how many opportunities they'll have to finally accept Christ; and no one knows if this moment is the last opportunity they'll have. God will forgive you for not accepting Christ the first time and He'll send other laborers across your path to bring you to Him, but never underestimate the devil that is set out to kill you. It's him who will stop at nothing to make sure you miss the next opportunity!

> The thief cometh not, but for to steal, and to kill, and to destroy: I am come that they might have life, and that they might have it more abundantly.—John 10:10

The angels of Heaven rejoice when a sinner repents and comes to Christ. The world tries to keep us from Him by offering us the earthly desires of our heart, but Heaven is forever and the Kingdom of Jesus begins in us now! If you've recently accepted Jesus as Lord and Savior, don't allow your faith battery to run out; start recharging it immediately! Love God with all of your heart because He loves you. Keep that faith alive by making Christ your first priority and His gospel your only mission in life. Make PSW your daily devotion.

> And thou shalt love the Lord thy God with all thy heart, and with all thy soul, and with all thy mind, and with all thy strength: this is the first commandment.—Mark 12:30

The Real You

It's amazing how much we learn when we study the Bible and how some of the messages jump right out at us when we read with a hungry heart. The scriptures are God's own inspired words that He's given to us so we can learn about Him and become better disciples. As we study, our faith grows and we feel confident that God loves us and will help us through anything. Yet—it's not until we attempt to put our faith to work that we really know how much of what we have read is in us. It's not until trials hit that we often discover who we really are.

It's easy to say, "Oh, I would never do that", or "If that happened to me I'd do this", but it's not always the way we react during an actual crisis. When we look at any conflict from the outside with an analytical eye, most of us would make a proper and calm decision. But when we're under pressure with unexpected trials, it's often an entirely different scenario. It's these trials that show us how much faith we have and what we believe—and how we will act.

Too often it's that down-to-earth, high-spirited and Bible filled person that shows a different face under pressure. The same guy who attends church on Sunday and leaves everyone envious of His remarkable faith and walk with God can become a tyrannical monster on a busy highway during rush hour. He demonstrates a nasty temper and allows his mouth to resort to old worldly habits as he shouts out threats and jerks his car forward to cut off surrounding traffic. How different he is from the Christian we see on Sunday's!

As we press forward to know God and serve Him with a whole heart, He allows trials to come that will test us along the way. And in each of these situations we have the ability to turn to God for help and to be the person we think we are—or not. Without these trials, we will never really know what we believe in our heart or how we will react to them in relation to what we've learned in the Bible. We need these trials so we can prove to our self what we've absorbed so far. It's the only way we'll really know who we are.

> There hath no temptation taken you but such as is common to man: but God is faithful, who will not suffer you to be tempted above that ye are able; but will with the temptation also make a way to escape, that ye may be able to bear it.—1 Corinthians 10:13

If we are short of money to pay a bill and we get angry and frustrated because we believe that we won't be able to pay it and risk facing a bad outcome because of it, that should tell us that we don't have faith in God to provide our needs. He said He would; we accepted it when we read it, but we don't trust Him to do it.

> But my God shall supply all your need according to his riches in glory by Christ Jesus.—Philippians 4:19

If we receive bad news and let depression take over with a sense of hopelessness, then we don't have the joy in our heart that we thought we had. We become weak and sorrowful because of it and we let this situation steal the joy from us; a joy in the Lord that says He will care for us.

> The joy of the Lord is your strength.— Nehemiah 8:10

If we are sick and we give in to the reports of the doctor and don't seek God for healing because we believe the bad reports instead of what God has said, then this tells us that we don't trust God to heal us even though He said we were healed at the cross. It's one thing to read it and accept it; it's quite another thing to believe it and act on it. And since many people don't get healed, our thoughts tend to drift into the world instead of onto the Lord.

> But He was wounded for our transgressions, He was bruised for our iniquities: the chastisement of our peace was upon Him; and with His stripes we are healed.—Isaiah 53:5

The trials we face always present us with the ability to choose what our actions will be. In fact, we need these trials to conquer our own doubts so we can focus on God. We can worry over the situation and be defeated, or pray about it and trust God. It's during these times that we discover if what we thought we knew actually got down into our heart.

> And all things, whatsoever ye shall ask in prayer, believing, ye shall receive.—Matthew 21:22

Many Christians believe that once they're saved their life will be the epitome of good health, prosperity and many blessings. They look at trials as attacks from the devil only and won't accept any bad things in life. However, this is not what the Bible says because Jesus tells us that we will have trials and tribulations in life. We can expect them because we live in a corrupt world. And we need them to teach us and show us where our faith level is in the Lord.

> These things I have spoken unto you, that in me ye might have peace. In the world ye shall have tribulation: but be of good cheer; I have overcome the world.—John 16:33

God only allows these trials to cross our path because He wants us to grow in faith and He knows that we can only do that a bit at a time. There are prosperity preachers out there who are screaming at their congregation to have the faith to believe God for big, expensive gifts. But many of the people can barely believe God to give them the simple things they need. This doesn't come from God. He does not expect us or allow us to be tried for something that is way above our ability. He only allows trials to come at us that meet the level of faith that we're at so that we can overcome them.

God does not test us, but He does allow the devil to test us. The devil's purpose, of course, is to prove that we don't trust God, and God's allowance for it is to give us an opportunity to put our faith to work. Each trial we encounter shows us what we've learned and what we will trust God with. And through each trial we grow stronger in the Lord.

If we react badly and don't trust God, then we need to go to Him and ask for His forgiveness for our bad attitude and lack of faith, and then ask Him to help us. We need to praise Him and thank Him for His love and for His faithfulness, and then get in the scriptures and read them and get them into our heart so that we can know that we know them. Then we can turn to God and truly believe Him to help us in this situation. When our faith is put on the line, we need to do what we are expected to do—and that is to trust God!

And we'll grow in faith as each one makes us stronger and more dependent on God. Then the scriptures are written on our heart and we'll be the witness and the disciple God has called us to be—in the good times and in the bad.

> Let the word of Christ dwell in you richly in all wisdom; teaching and admonishing one another in psalms and hymns and spiritual songs, singing with grace in your hearts to the Lord.—Colossians 3:16

Who Do You Follow?

Choosing to be a Christian is the most significant and valuable decision that a person will ever make in his or her lifetime. There are a million different crossroads in life that bring people to this decision, and unfortunately, just as many false doctrines that will lead them away. If we are going to make it to Heaven, then we need to know from the onset who we will follow and who we will serve: Jesus or someone who proclaims to know Him.

It seems that today more and more people are falling into the pattern of following a person who supposedly follows Jesus. This way they don't have to study the Bible and they can depend on their leader to teach them everything that "they" want to know. After all, these different leaders all proclaim to follow Jesus and they teach all kinds of accepted ways of life. And so there's one out there for all the different so-called "Christians" so they can hear what suits them the best. However, this is not only foolish, but it's wrong according to the Bible.

There are many records in the New Testament where Jesus has told us to follow Him:

> Follow Me, and I will make you fishers of men.—Matthew 4:19

> And he who does not take his cross and follow after Me is not worthy of Me.— Matthew 10:38

> If anyone desires to come after Me, let him deny himself and take up his cross and follow Me."—Matthew 16:24 [i]

> One thing you lack: Go your way, sell whatever you have and give to the poor, and

> you will have treasure in heaven; and come, take up the cross, and follow Me.—Mark 10:21

> I am the light of the world. He who follows Me shall not walk in darkness, but have the light of life.—John 8:12

> My sheep hear My voice, and I know them, and they follow Me.—John 10:27

> If anyone serves Me, let him follow Me; and where I am, there My servant will be also. If anyone serves Me, him My Father will honor.—John 12:26

Nowhere in the Bible does God ever tell us to follow anyone except Him. In fact, when we choose to follow a person and trust them and honor them as our leader, what we are doing, in essence, is making that person our god. What does the Lord say about other gods? He says in Exodus 20:3, "You shall have no other gods before Me."

This is not to be confused with sitting under the leadership of our pastor because his job is to keep the eyes and hearts of the congregation on God. But even so, we need to be like the Bereans who Apostle Paul taught because they listened to the preaching and then searched the scriptures themselves to verify that what was being preached was the gospel of Christ. We shouldn't just take every word that anyone else says without studying the scriptures to prove it.

> And the brethren immediately sent away Paul and Silas by night unto Berea: who coming thither went into the synagogue of the Jews. 11 These were more noble than those in Thessalonica, in that they received the word with all readiness of mind, and searched the

scriptures daily, whether those things were so.—Acts 17:10-11

We need to study the Bible ourselves and get to know God. We need to learn who He is, what His laws are, who we are in Christ and what is expected of us as Christians. It means that we become responsible for our own salvation and that we don't depend on someone else to get us to Heaven. Apostle Paul emphasises this important point.

> Wherefore, my beloved, as ye have always obeyed, not as in my presence only, but now much more in my absence, work out your own salvation with fear and trembling.— Philippians 2:12

This doesn't mean that we do any kind of works to get saved because salvation comes through faith, not by works. Our salvation is given to us by God when He gives that initial gift of faith to believe that Jesus came from Heaven, lived on earth as a humble man and then was nailed to the cross because He was the Lamb of God and ultimate sacrifice for our sins. He is Holy and without sin, and He took upon Himself all of our sins and removed the curse of the law from us so that we are no longer under the law, but under grace. We all deserved the punishment for our sins, but He took those sins from us and forgave us and restored us back to God and gave to us His Holy Spirit. No person can reveal this truth to us. The only way we'll get this truth planted in our heart is to prayerfully study the Bible and let God reveal it to us.

> For what man knows the things of a man except the spirit of the man which is in him? Even so no one knows the things of God except the Spirit of God.—1 Corinthians 2:11 NKJV

Lead me in Your truth and teach me, For You
are the God of my salvation; On You I wait
all the day—Psalm 25:5 NKJV

We need to study and get this truth deep into our soul
so that we can know beyond a shadow of a doubt who God
is, who Jesus is, and who we are in Jesus and what lies ahead
for us. And when we follow Jesus and study His Word [the
Bible] then we will know the truth and the truth shall make
us free—John 8:32.

But deception is a powerful tool! The devil uses it to
fool us into thinking that we're on the right path when we
aren't. And the easiest way to do this is to send people across
our path whose version of the gospel caters more to the flesh
than to the spirit, and if we don't know the truth then we will
be deceived. Maybe the people we follow are right on the
line with the gospel, but we won't know that if we don't take
the time to prove it by studying the scriptures prayerfully on
our own. We put ourselves on a very dangerous path when
our trust is in a person instead of in God personally. If we
don't verify the truth for ourselves, we can easily be deceived
into believing a lie because we trust the person teaching us
more than we trust ourselves to prove it.

Being a Christian is not about us; it's about Jesus. It's
about following Jesus and being part of who He is and
sharing the gospel with others so they can know Him, too.
This gospel is the "good news message" about the salvation
that God has for us and the reward of being with Him in
Heaven throughout eternity. It's also a warning for those who
don't know Him that their destination is judgment and
punishment with an eternity in total darkness engulfed in
corruption and evil—apart from God.

When we love Jesus, we follow Him with joy and our
heart yearns to hear His voice in the scriptures. But when we

follow people and don't search for the truth ourselves, we take a risk that we might regret. It seems easier to just follow a person and trust that what they're saying is accurate, but isn't your eternal life worth being sure?

> For the time will come when they will not endure sound doctrine, but according to their own desires, because they have itching ears, they will heap up for themselves teachers; 4 and they will turn their ears away from the truth, and be turned aside to fables.—2 Timothy 4:3-4 NKJV

People can guide us, pray with us, encourage us and inspire us, but the only one we should follow and subject our life to is Jesus! Yet, many don't, and so we have different gospels and millions of so-called "Christians" following people and their version of the scriptures. And they're following them down that broad path right behind the great deceiver himself, the devil—Matthew 7:13-14.

Who do you follow, Jesus or someone who proclaims to know Him? Your decision is crucial and your future depends on it!

> And if it seems evil to you to serve the Lord, choose for yourselves this day whom you will serve, whether the gods which your fathers served that were on the other side of the River, or the gods of the Amorites, in whose land you dwell. But as for me and my house, we will serve the Lord.—Joshua 24:15

Wimp or Warrior

As Christians, we pray and take our issues to God and hope that He will give us the wisdom or open some door so we can get the victory over our trials. Some pray and never seem to get an answer while others pray and the answer comes and everyone knows that God answered their prayer. Why do some prayers get answered and not others? Perhaps there's a difference in who is praying: a wimp or a warrior.

What is prayer?

Prayer is our communication with our Heavenly Father. And contrary to what many people think, it's far more than just asking Him for things—repeatedly. When we get together with our earthly father, we don't just give him a list of things that we want every time we visit him. We talk with him, laugh and cry with him, and share news with him. We tell him that we love him and we thank him for the things that he does for us because we know that he loves us. We may tell him about things we need, but we don't make that our focal point for each visit. In other words, we have a personal relationship with our earthly father that is based on love and trust.

And so is our visit with our Heavenly Father. Prayer is our personal time with Him and we talk about many things. We'll confess things to Him that we did or didn't do and we'll ask for His forgiveness. We talk to Him about others who need His help and ask for His divine intervention in their lives. We thank Him for His faithfulness toward us and for His love and for His blessings. We praise Him for His grace and for His patients and for Him meeting our needs and answering the prayers for others. And yes, when we have needs, or even desires, we tell Him about them. Prayer time is our time to just be with our Father.

> Be careful for nothing; but in everything by
> prayer and supplication with thanksgiving let
> your requests be made known unto God.—
> Philippians 4:6

A weak (or wimpy) prayer is one that lacks
confidence and trust in God, and comes from not having a
relationship with Him. Many Christians pray to God and ask
Him for the same things that they asked Him for the day
before. Their prayer wasn't answered so they assume they
have to keep on asking. But there is one important thing to
know about God—He has a perfect memory! And you don't
need to ask Him twice because He also has perfect hearing
and He heard you the first time.

People get confused with the scriptures that tell us to
bring our requests before Him and they think that it means to
ask Him for the same things over and over. But we don't
need to constantly "ask" Him for things. We ask in prayer
once and then bring that issue up to Him as often as we want,
BUT not as a request! We bring it to Him and thank Him for
hearing us and for answering us. We praise Him that He is
Almighty God who CAN and who WILL answer our prayer.
We ask Him once and praise Him often!

What separates a weak prayer person from a prayer
warrior? Relationship! Prayer warriors know their Heavenly
Father. They know the Bible and they know what God said
about things. Through their studying of the scriptures and
their time spent in prayer and worship, they have grown to
know God. Not just "about" God, but they actually "know"
Him and have developed a relationship "with" Him.

Prayer warriors can pray in confidence because they
know what their Father has said and has promised and they
believe it. They know what things are the will of God and so
they can pray confidently, knowing that they are praying in

sync with what God has said in the Bible. They have no doubt AND they also know that God's ways are not our ways, so if a prayer isn't answered exactly the way we expected, they are not surprised because they trust God's ways.

> For my thoughts are not your thoughts, neither are your ways my ways, saith the Lord.—Isaiah 55:8

Prayer warriors have knowledge and confidence in what they are praying about. They are humble before God, not arrogant or demanding. They come to God with thanksgiving, knowing fully that the Lord is in control of everything and that no one is greater or wiser, or is fairer or more knowledgeable, or more forgiving or more loving than He is. They know that they are His children, not His equal.

Before Jesus did any of the miracles that He did on earth, He always prayed to His Heavenly Father first. He didn't need to because He had the power to do it all, but He set an example for us. We also should pray and thank God for taking care of us, and we should give Him all the glory, knowing that He can and will answer our requests.

> And He commanded the multitude to sit down on the grass, and took the five loaves, and the two fishes, and looking up to heaven, He blessed, and break, and gave the loaves to His disciples, and the disciples to the multitude.— Matthew 14:19

When Jesus came to the cave where Lazarus was buried, He didn't just rush in and raise him from the dead. Jesus first prayed and thanked His Heavenly Father and then went in. His example tells us that we have to know God, and know what He will do, and then we will have the confidence in Him to thank Him for doing it.

> Then they took away the stone from the place
> where the dead was laid. And Jesus lifted up
> his eyes, and said, 'Father, I thank thee that
> thou hast heard me.'—John 11:41

Prayer warriors know who their enemy is! And they know that Jesus has already defeated that enemy on the cross! They walk by faith (in Christ) and not by sight (the situation at hand). They stay focused on the fact that God is in charge and that He alone is working on the answer.

Weak Christians only hope that God will answer them. They don't know His will, but they hope that what they are asking for is okay. They keep their eyes on the issues and walk by sight while hoping to see it change as soon as possible. They don't have the faith, the trust, or the confidence in God to be able to just leave it with Him and know that He's working on the problem.

Prayer warriors know that they are not fighting on their own turf. They know that their enemy is one who can trick them and deceive them into thinking that he has the power to defeat them. They know that God has the power over the devil and that when we resist him he will leave.

> For we wrestle not against flesh and blood,
> but against principalities, against powers,
> against the rulers of the darkness of this
> world, against spiritual wickedness in high
> places.—Ephesians 6:12

Prayer warriors know that light and dark cannot be in the same place at the same time, and when they pray they bring the presence of God into the situation and things happen! Why? Because when they pray and praise God for the answer, the devil leaves as he cannot stand to be in the presence of worship.

Submit yourselves therefore to God. Resist the devil, and he will flee from you.—James 4:7

Prayer warriors know that they need to put on the full armour of God to be able to stand against the devil and his tricks. No one goes into a battle field without any weapons— even King David had a sling shot! And so we must prepare ourselves and be ready to stand against the enemy!

Put on the whole armour of God that ye may be able to stand against the wiles of the devil. 12 For we wrestle not against flesh and blood, but against principalities, against powers, against the rulers of the darkness of this world, against spiritual wickedness in high places. 13 Wherefore take unto you the whole armour of God that ye may be able to withstand in the evil day, and having done all, to stand. 14 Stand therefore, having your loins girt about with truth, and having on the breastplate of righteousness; 15 And your feet shod with the preparation of the gospel of peace; 16 Above all, taking the shield of faith, wherewith ye shall be able to quench all the fiery darts of the wicked. 17 And take the helmet of salvation, and the sword of the Spirit, which is the word of God: 18 Praying always with all prayer and supplication in the Spirit, and watching thereunto with all perseverance and supplication for all saints.— Ephesians 6:11-18

Words are not Enough

It seems as if the world is becoming saturated with people proclaiming to be Christians, yet there are no obvious fruits in their lives to reflect that they are. The truth is that not everyone who calls him or herself a Christian is one. There's more to being a Christian than just saying you're one. Words need to be put into action because in this world where people are watching, words alone are not enough.

There's a lot more to being a Christian than going to church on Sunday's and habitually placing our offerings into the basket. It's more than giving others a hug and sending them off with, "God bless you". And it's more than hanging out with a Christian crowd during the week and even attending Christian concerts on the weekends. These all give the appearance of a good person, someone who is likely a Christian. But looks alone can be deceiving.

A real Christian bears fruit. Our personality, characteristics and actions reflect those of Jesus. This is what separates us from the people of the world. We are different. We read in 1 Peter 2:9, "But ye are a chosen generation, a royal priesthood, an holy nation, a peculiar people; that ye should shew forth the praises of Him who hath called you out of darkness into his marvellous light." We don't blend in with the world and we don't hide who we are. We don't need to tell people that we're a Christian; the way we live and act will testify to them that we are.

> But the fruit of the Spirit is love, joy, peace, longsuffering, gentleness, goodness, faith, 23 Meekness, temperance: against such there is no law.—Galatians 5:22-23

The fruits we bear should be visible in everything we do, not just in what we say. We can't proclaim to be a Christian and not bear the fruit because it's the fruit or the

254

"characteristics of Christ in us" that reassures us that God's Holy Spirit lives in us. And it's ONLY through His Spirit in us that the world will ever see God in this present time. We need to put our faith to work because if we don't, it's dead — James 2:20—and no one will see Jesus working through us.

Apostle Paul tells us that we are to live like Christ and that His values and His character should be in us. He instructs us to turn from the world and in doing so we will not want the world's ways to be in us anymore. We will want to be and act like Jesus because His Spirit lives in us.

> For ye were sometimes darkness, but now are ye light in the Lord: walk as children of light: 9 (For the fruit of the Spirit is in all goodness and righteousness and truth;) 10 Proving what is acceptable unto the Lord.—Ephesians 5:8-10

So if we are going to be like Jesus, then we need to develop our character by reading the four gospels in the New Testament (Matthew, Mark, Luke and John) and allowing God's Holy Spirit who dwells in us, to teach us in all truth. Then as we study, we will take on the personality and characteristics—or fruits—of the Spirit of God. We will learn that Jesus did far more than just send well wishes to people. Jesus was a servant! And He expects us to serve others with the same passion and love for God that He showed to us during His earthly ministry. And He's given to us His Spirit to work through us in the same way that His Spirit worked through Him.

> So after he had washed their feet, and had taken his garments, and was set down again, he said unto them, 'Know ye what I have done to you? 13 Ye call me Master and Lord: and ye say well; for so I am. 14 If I then, your

Lord and Master, have washed your feet; ye
also ought to wash one another's feet. 15 For I
have given you an example, that ye should do
as I have done to you. 16 Verily, verily, I say
unto you, The servant is not greater than his
lord; neither he that is sent greater than he that
sent him. 17 If ye know these things, happy
are ye if ye do them.'— John 13:12-17

When we are saved we literally go from having the
nature of the world inside us to having it removed and being
replaced by God's Spirit. But it doesn't stop there. We need
to study the Bible and let His Spirit teach us about God
because as Christians, we are on a mission to get others
saved. The passions of Christ and the knowledge of God
need to flow through us and onto the people of this hurting
world. Jesus tells us to let our light shine so the world can see
Him. The only way the world is going to get saved is through
Jesus, and so we need to draw people to Him by letting His
Spirit live through us as a light onto a dark world. And we
don't do this by being a quiet Sunday Christian. We do this
by our works!

Let your light so shine before men, that they
may see your good works, and glorify your
Father which is in heaven.—Matthew 5:16

It is only through God's Holy Spirit in us that we can
be that light and that we can fulfill God's mission for us here
on earth.

For we are his workmanship, created in Christ
Jesus unto good works, which God hath
before ordained that we should walk in
them.—Ephesians 2:10

There are many ways that we can reveal God's love to people and win souls for Christ. We can show it in our daily lives to our neighbors, to the people at the local grocery stores, to our co-workers, and to anyone and everyone we come in contact with during the day. Everything we do will reflect what Jesus did when He lived here on earth, and they'll become a natural part of our life. We won't need to focus on what we should do because we'll just do it and God will give us the words to speak when we need them.

We'll take great joy in supporting other Christian ministries who are out on the front lines fighting battles and witnessing to the ungodly and feeding the poor; all the things that need to be done, but that we can't get out and do. We'll know what ministries are good and which ones are false because the ones of God will preach the gospel of Christ. Their only purpose will be to get souls saved and to help the downtrodden, and the people within them won't expect to receive earthly rewards for their works. They won't be smothered with riches and teach how to get more; they'll be out there working, sharing, getting dirty and being persecuted because they come in the name of our Lord.

Such ministries include Samaritan's Purse, which is made up of Christian volunteers around the globe who go into disaster areas to help the victims get their lives put back together. Some of us can be a volunteer, others can send funding—and all of us can pray!

Then there's the Paul Wilbur Ministries; this man has devoted his life to God and to sharing the gospel with the Jewish people first and then the Gentiles, and he does this through his inspiring worship music and his powerful messages of the gospel. The Billy Graham Ministry with Franklin Graham and others of the Graham family preach the gospel to America and around the world, and warn the people to get ready because Jesus is coming soon. Jay Sekalow is a devoted Christian lawyer whose organization fights for the legal rights of people around the world. They battle day and night for the freedom of imprisoned Christians, for God's laws not to be changed into corruption and for the lives of innocent babies to be saved from abortion.

These are all ministries working in different areas of humanity, but all to the glory of God. These aren't prosperity teachers or mega-churches that preach carnal messages for the "modern day Christian", but these are people who put their lives on the line every day because the love of God is in them and they want to get people saved. Most of us can't be part of any of these physical teams, but we sure can support them with our finances and our prayers.

Being a Christian is what life is all about and it's not enough to just say we are one; we need to think, act, speak and pray like one! We serve God with a whole heart by serving people and helping them to find God as well as helping them through their problems. That means sharing whatever we have to share and not hoarding it for ourselves for some time in the future. We're not looking for rewards here on earth and we're not looking to be recognized by people. We do what we do to the glory of God, and our reward is in Heaven when Jesus opens His arms and says,

> Well done, thou good and faithful servant: thou hast been faithful over a few things, I will make thee ruler over many things: enter thou into the joy of thy lord.—Matthew 25:21

Treasures of the Heart

One of the things that many of us in the civilized world pride ourselves in is our collection of worldly goods. Some of us have the funds to back our expensive desires and others of us struggle to acquire even a few over a lifetime. But the fact is, most of us can look around our homes and see things that we cherish because they are the treasures of our heart and have great material worth. But in the end, they are worth nothing at all.

They appease our desire when we are able to appreciate them, but they come with a cost. Not only the financial cost of the things themselves, but we have to put insurance on them and then worry in case they get broken if touched, or damaged in any way through any number of disasters that could happen. We guard these collectibles throughout our lifetime and put them into bright showcases for everyone to see. Yes, we are proud of our collection. But the truth is, they are worthless.

God tells us to put our treasures into Heavenly things because they are the only things that have value. We can't take any of these earthly treasures with us when we die no matter what effort and money was put in to getting them. They have value here on earth, but mostly to those who value them as treasures.

> Lay not up for yourselves treasures upon earth, where moth and rust doth corrupt, and where thieves break through and steal: 20 But lay up for yourselves treasures in heaven, where neither moth nor rust doth corrupt, and where thieves do not break through nor steal: 21 For where your treasure is, there will your heart be also. —Matthew 6:19-21

Ronnie Dauber

Last year I attended a funeral for a dear Christian woman and it was then that I realized the true value of life and how so many of us waste our time and money collecting things that have no eternal value. During her lifetime, she had accumulated many extraordinary and beautiful treasures. When she became ill and had to move from her home to a long-term care facility, she was initially concerned about her valuable things. She took as many as she could with her and her family packed the rest away. But as her health began to fail, she lost concern for her "things" and soon forgot that she even had them. When anyone mentioned them to her, she shrugged it off and eventually she didn't even recognize the ones she'd brought with her. She lost all value for the things that she had worked so hard to attain and protect during her lifetime, and the only thing that mattered to her in the end was going to Heaven to be with Jesus—her true treasure.

> In my Father's house are many mansions: if it were not so, I would have told you. I go to prepare a place for you. 3 And if I go and prepare a place for you, I will come again, and receive you unto myself; that where I am, there ye may be also.—John 14:2-3

The things that many consider to be treasures in their homes mean everything to those who collect them, and the hard truth is that these same "things" often don't have any great material value to others. We spend a lifetime collecting things and in the end, they are worthless to us and often to those around us. These "valuables" can't improve our health or add one second of time to our life, nor can they bring us closer to God or even make death any easier. They are "things" and they belong to this world, and not only can't we can't take them with us, we don't want to.

Sometimes our values get twisted and we focus more on our own needs and desires than we do on the needs of

260

others. Sometimes we get so caught up with filling our homes with good things that we forget to notice what others don't have; what others need. We can never allow our eyes to deliberately avoid those around us because if we love God we will want to help and bless others with the same integrity that God bless us.

> But whoso hath this world's good, and seeth his brother have need, and shutteth up his bowels of compassion from him, how dwelleth the love of God in him?—1 John 3:17

God has treasures beyond our imagination waiting for us in Heaven and they have no connection whatsoever to anything on this earth. The things in this world are temporal; the things that God has for us in Heaven will last throughout eternity and we will love them, cherish them and praise God for them.

> But as it is written, 'Eye hath not seen, nor ear heard, neither have entered into the heart of man, the things which God hath prepared for them that love him.'—1 Corinthians 2:9

This doesn't mean that we can't enjoy some of the nice material possessions of this world now while we're here. God wants us to be happy and He likes to bless us. He tells us in Psalm 37:4, "Delight thyself also in the Lord: and He shall give thee the desires of thine heart." And while we will appreciate these material things that make our life more enjoyable, at no point will they ever become our earthy treasure; they will always be blessings from God. So as long as we have them, we'll be content and if we lose them we'll be just as content because we know that it's God who gives these blessings to His children. And if He wants us to have them, He'll give them to us again. And if these blessings

261

become too important to us, we need to realize that He just might take them away.

And as long as we know in our heart that these "things" belong to this world, and that we will never make these "material possessions" our treasures, we can have the things we ask God for. And He'll give them to us because He knows our heart, and He knows that our love for Him is far greater than these possessions and that they will never be challenged by anything this earth has to offer.

Our goal as Christians in this time should be getting into Heaven and bowing to the One who made it possible for us to be there. And although the things of this world will never get into Heaven, there is one type of treasure that we can collect and take with us! And they are worth everything to God and to us here and in Heaven! And these treasures are the souls who we have won for Christ. These are the ones who we have prayed for, and, witnessed to and lead into salvation. These are our treasures that God will reward us for as we're given the Crown of Rejoicing, sometimes referred to as "the soul-winner's crown". These are the riches that bring glory to God and that make up the "treasures" of Heaven.

These are the treasures that we need to collect throughout our life. There is nothing more valuable to God than having His children come home, and if our goal is to please God because we love Him, then it will be our goal to help others find their way to Him, as well. Whether we are serving on the frontlines or being a prayer warrior in the background, getting others saved is the greatest treasure that any Christian could seek after. And it's one that we will have throughout eternity with Jesus!

> For what is our hope, or joy, or crown of rejoicing? Are not even ye in the presence of

our Lord Jesus Christ at his coming?—1
Thessalonians 2:19

We can't take any earthly thing that we have with us
when we leave this world, and even though they bring us
pleasure while we're here, they still belong to this world.
And nothing of this world can compare to the blessings that
the Lord has for us in Heaven.

For where your treasure is, there will your
heart be also. —Matthew 6:21

Ronnie Dauber

Responding to God's Call

In these last days as Christ gets ready to return, the devil is working hard to deceive many and keep them from accepting God in their heart. The new age "Christianity" is designed to satisfy the lusts of the flesh and trick the mind into thinking that it's the real thing. There are many seemingly godly men and women who teach false doctrines and make it sound real. People follow these leaders who call them into their fold and they blindly enter into the religion of this world and think that it's God calling them. But it isn't.

God does call people—Matthew 22:14—but God only uses the truth in His scriptures that are revealed to us through His own Spirit. Anything else is false! And those who follow after people and not after the true gospel won't seek God for themselves, and they'll follow down the path that seems more appealing.

We know that as Christians we'll suffer persecutions because as we read earlier, Jesus warned us about them. We can't speak against the ruler of this world and in favor of his greatest enemy—Jesus—and not experience any resistance. But the battle isn't ours; it belongs to the Lord and all we have to do is seek His face and follow His instructions.

Once we're saved, we have God on our side and there is nothing that we can't do to fulfill His great commission. We don't go on our own strength because we can't fight against the powers of darkness on our own strength. But we have His Spirit in us who teaches us and guides us and ministers to us and makes us wise, knowledgeable and strong. What love our Heavenly Father has for us!

If God be for us, who can be against us?—
Romans 8:31

This book was written to make people aware of some of the decoys and deceptions that are plaguing the Christian world today to keep them from knowing the truth. If you want to come out of it and belong to God's kingdom, then just go to Him in prayer because His arms are wide open and ready to receive you. It does NOT matter what you've done in your lifetime or what sins you have committed because when you come to Jesus and give it all to Him, He truly takes it away and all of it is forgiven.

And when you come to the Lord, you likely won't hear thunder or see lightning flashes, but you will feel His peace and you will know that you know that something inside you is different. And though you might not see them, the angels in Heaven will rejoice because God says that they rejoice over every sinner who comes to Him and repents.

> I say unto you, that likewise joy shall be in heaven over one sinner that repenteth, more than over ninety and nine just persons, which need no repentance. 8 Either what woman having ten pieces of silver, if she lose one piece, doth not light a candle, and sweep the house, and seek diligently till she find it? 9 And when she hath found it, she calleth her friends and her neighbours together, saying, Rejoice with me; for I have found the piece which I had lost. 10 Likewise, I say unto you, there is joy in the presence of the angels of God over one sinner that repenteth.—Luke 15:7-10

We have all sinned and come short of the glory of God—Romans 3:23—and so we all must come to God in prayer and repent so we can be born again. And for the rest of our earthly lives we will be aware of His power and glory and of our weakness and humility. We will all makes mistakes or slip into an old habit or just do something that is wrong once in a while, and we'll all need to come to Him and ask for forgiveness again. And as His children, as Christians who have been grafted into His kingdom, we have the confidence that He forgives us and will continue to live in us until that great day when He calls us home.

The "sinner's prayer" should not be rehearsed or spoken in big words that we don't understand. They should be words that reflect what's in our heart because it's our heart that is crying out to God. We ask Him to forgive us and to fill us with His Spirit so that we can live for Him.

Whether you're coming to the cross for the first time, or coming to God with a sorrowful heart because you fell into the teaching of a false doctrine, He will hear you and He will forgive you if you mean it.

Don't delay your salvation. If you're reading this, then take it as an opportunity that God has given to you to come to Him. Now is the time to receive the Lord.

God is calling YOU!

Behold, now is the accepted time; behold, now is the day of salvation.

—2 Corinthians 6:2

About the Author

Ronnie Dauber is a Canadian Christian author whose commitment is to share the gospel of Jesus with others. Her passion is to reveal God's truth through her books and her blog, to share God's amazing grace and love with others, and to open their eyes to the deceptions of false doctrines that will keep them from knowing the true God of Heaven.

Ronnie also enjoys writing novels for young adults as she wants to encourage them to read exciting books that are packed with action and suspense, yet totally void of profanity and sexual content. Her *Sarah Davies* series has four titles to date: Mudslide, Firestorm, Whiteout and Raging Waters.

She is currently working on her fifth inspirational book, *The Last King,* to be released by the fall of 2016. It's about the return of our Lord and Savior, King Jesus, and it analyzes the signs of His return that Jesus told us to look for in Matthew 24. It's easy to read and to understand so you can realize that the return of our King is closer than you think!

Ms. Dauber lives in Canada with her husband, children and grand children.

You can read more of her inspirational messages on her blog:

Smile, God Loves You!
http://www.ronniedauber.com

Smile, God Loves You!